HOW TO BE GORGEOUS

FIONA FODEN
ILLUSTRATED BY GERI COADY

For Erin

Scholastic Children's Books,
Euston House, 24 Eversholt Street,
London NW1 1DB, UK

A division of Scholastic Ltd
London ~ New York ~ Toronto ~ Sydney ~ Auckland
Mexico City ~ New Delhi ~ Hong Kong

Published in the UK by Scholastic Ltd, 2012

ISBN 978 1407 13269 3

Printed and bound by CPI Group (UK) Ltd, Croydon CR0 4YY

2 4 6 8 10 9 7 5 3 1

CONTENTS

What's this book all about?

It's about how to be gorgeous — that's obvious, right? Yet there's so much more to gorgeousness than glossy hair, glowing skin or a to-die-for dress (although these all help, of course). It's not even about looking like a supermodel, a pop star or having those weird, zingy-white teeth like just about everyone on TV. It's about looking amazing, but still being you.

Did you know you can think yourself gorgeous? It's about having the confidence to believe in yourself, with the kind of positive, 'buzzy' energy that helps you get the most out of life. In fact, that's often a lot more powerful than appearance alone. In other words, true gorgeousness is more than skin deep.

It's also about having lovely friends and the best times ever — that's what makes life truly gorgeous. Whether it's creating a beautiful bedroom, hosting a brilliant sleepover or putting together a fabulous look from what's already hiding away in your wardrobe — these are the kind of things that sprinkle a little gorgeousness over everyday life.

It's not hard, it won't break the bank — in fact, many of the ideas in this handy little book are virtually free. And they're all easy — that's an absolute promise. So why not get started right now? Your gorgeous life awaits …

PS ... Just so you know, there are a few points in this book where you'll need to use the hob or the oven to make your own beauty products, or yummy treats. Please ask for help if you need it and remember that gorgeous girls are always careful.

How to be confident

If there's one special quality that makes inner gorgeousness shine through, it's confidence.

Feeling good about yourself makes you more relaxed about getting to know new people, more secure in your own self, and less likely to crumble when someone says something mean. It also helps you to recover quickly when you suffer a set-back or a big disappointment. Confidence is a sort of super-power. It makes you feel bold, brave and daring, so you're more likely to try new things, make new friends and do your very best — because you believe you can do it.

Ah, but where does confidence come from? How can you find it within yourself and encourage it to grow and blossom like an incredible flower? Try these ...

Ten Confidence Commandments

1. Don't worry about what other people think. While it's natural to be aware of how you come across to others, don't let those niggling thoughts clog up too much of your brain-space. Singer Adele, a fine example of inner and outer gorgeousness, puts it this way: 'I've found that, when I doubt myself, I'm concentrating on what other people are thinking of me rather than what I think of myself.'

2. Believe in yourself. When presented with something challenging to do, don't think, 'Help! What if I mess up?' – that just makes you want to hide in a corner or run away. Instead, tell yourself, 'Lots of people do this all the time. I'm a clever and capable person – that means I can do it too.' Another handy tactic is to act as if you know exactly what you're doing. This tricks the brain into thinking, 'I can do this,' rather than, '*Aargh* – get me out of here!'

3. Do something that makes you feel a little bit scared. There's nothing like overcoming a challenge to make your confidence grow. Feisty actress Kristen Stewart always picks film roles that stretch her: 'I choose things that are so overly ambitious, and if I can't do stuff like that, I don't want to be doing this,' she says.

4. Start with a small challenge, then work up to a bigger one. For instance, try singing in a group before performing all on your own. This approach is called 'taking baby steps', and it gives your confidence the chance to grow as you manage each new challenge beautifully.

5. Remember that no one feels 100% confident all the time. After all, that would be pretty unbearable! As Pixie Lott puts it: 'Even if you're a shy person, you can be lovely with it. I have days when I'm tired and I can't be bothered to talk as much — but confidence grows every year.'

6. If something goes wrong, don't dwell on it. Just brush it aside and move on to something else instead.

7. Ignore people who put you down. They're probably just attention seeking or deeply envious, so why let them stop you succeeding?

8. Accept praise with a smile. Don't do the automatic thing of muttering, 'Oh, I'm rubbish really.' Okay, you don't want to seem boastful either, so just smile, say 'thanks' and hold on to that praise for a moment. People rarely give positive feedback when it's not truly deserved.

9. Store a small, secret 'library' of positive thoughts in your head. That way, you can draw on them when you feel a bit wobbly. These thoughts should be about things you know you're good at: for instance, 'I'm friendly and approachable,' 'I'm good at concentrating and have a brilliant imagination,' 'I'm organized and thoughtful.'

10. Never forget for an instant how unique and fantastic you are. If you don't hold that thought in your head, who will?

How to make a trend work for you

So all your friends have adopted a trend, but you're not sure it's right for you. It's always best to follow your instincts on matter of style, rather than splurging all your money (or begging someone else to) on something that never feels right. Here's a quick checklist of questions to ask yourself before you make the latest trend yours:

Do I actually like this trend? Or am I being drawn to it because everyone else is wearing it and it's in all the magazines?

Is it a bit ugly or mad-looking? Do I really want to look like this?

Will I feel comfortable wearing this shape/style/colour? And will I be able to do the things I love to do while I'm wearing it? Never wear something you don't feel good in just because it's fashionable.

Then, if you're satisfied that it's something you do want to play around with, you can politely introduce it into your wardrobe ('Wardrobe, meet new trend …') in one of these ways:

Add just a nod to the trend with animal print/fluorescent/lace (or whichever trend is hot right now) accessory rather than a head-to-toe look. That way, you won't look as if you're slavishly following fashion, yet will still feel on-trend and stylish. It's a budget-friendly approach too.

Add just one piece, such as a top, and wear it with the usual clothes you feel 100% relaxed and confident in. That way, the trend fits into your style, rather than the other way round.

Borrow a piece from a friend and give it a 'test drive' by wearing it out and about, to see if it feels right for you.

Of course, just because a trend is everywhere doesn't mean you have to adopt it. Some trends are fabulous, flattering and fun. And some are utterly bonkers and end up on the 70% off rail in a few months' time. By this point, the style-slaves in your group will be cringing at pictures of themselves wearing it, while you've breezed through the past few months looking fabulously relaxed – and, most vitally, like you.

How to have silky, swishy hair

While the whole hair business can seem horribly complicated, it doesn't have to be. The main things hair needs are nourishment and a whole lot of love (well, who doesn't?). Fussy, fiddly 'dos can be fun if you've got the time to experiment, but worrying about your hair, and constantly checking if it looks okay, is a complete pain. And you've got far better things to do with your life than that.

Luckily, all you need for truly gorgeous hair are these five brilliantly easy steps:

Cut ...

You might have heard that having your hair cut makes it grow thicker. While that's not actually true, it does look (and feel) thicker when it's freshly cut, because all those wispy ends have been snipped away. Every couple of months is ideal, although shorter styles need more frequent trims.

Wash ...

You know your own hair. It might seem to 'need' a wash every day, but sometimes hair looks better the day after. Just shampoo as often as you feel your hair requires it (and every day is fine, if it's looking good and not too dry). There's no need for posh shampoos containing fancy ingredients like orchid essence or truffle oil. A mild, gentle shampoo generally does the job brilliantly, without any fuss.

Feed ...

Well, *condition* really, which means nourishing from root to tip. A combined shampoo-conditioner means one less bottle to trip over in the shower, but you'll generally see better results with a separate conditioner. Turn off the shower and slightly towel dry your hair after washing, then massage conditioner through your hair, from the roots to the ends where it tends to be driest. Leave it on for a minute or so — honestly, this makes all the difference. Then rinse until it's squeaky clean (lingering conditioner makes hair dull) and revel in its new-found silkiness.

Feed more ...

Because hair can be a little bit greedy. An occasional deep-conditioning treatment is a lovely pampering treat, especially if you've been swimming loads, or on the beach where salt water can trigger a frizz attack. These treatments are basically ultra-rich conditioners that either come in tubs or sachets — once or twice a week is quite enough. Apply to towel-dried hair just like normal conditioner, then bundle up your hair in a towel, like a turban. You can then float around in your bedroom, feeling exotic, for ten minutes or so before hopping back in the shower and rinsing off. Then dry as normal. (Remember to put that towel straight in the wash.)

Brush ...

100 brush strokes a day was recommended in the olden days, but what modern girl has time for that? Do take care to brush thoroughly right to the ends though. This distributes your hair's natural oils and boosts shine. You'll get best results with a fairly posh brush that has natural bristles.

If your hair's still looking a bit 'bleurgh' …

Maybe you're washing it too often and stripping away the natural oils that give hair its gloss. Try shampooing every second day instead of daily. Find your hair's ideal wash schedule and stick with that.

Your regular shampoo and/or conditioner might not suit your hair. Try a different brand (it needn't be expensive) and see if it makes a difference.

Girls with curly or wavy hair often wish theirs was dead straight, and straight-haired girls usually crave a bit of a wave – but never forget that you're gorgeous just as you are. Using hair straighteners means an awful lot of heat on your hair, which can be drying and damaging. It's best to limit them for special occasions only, and always use a heat protector product too. Can you believe that girls in the 1950s used to iron their hair, with a normal iron? Highly dangerous, and their poor hair ended up frazzled too. Thankfully, you know better …

How to have a gorgeous smile

A gorgeous smile is natural and always reaches your eyes. It's never forced or fake, which means that the loveliest smile – one that really lights up your face – happens when you feel genuinely happy and good about yourself, and not remotely self-conscious.

So really, the less you worry about your smile, the more gorgeous it will be. In the meantime, if your confidence needs a little boost, try these to get your teeth looking their best:

Powered toothbrushes (the kind that usually have a rechargeable battery) clean really well, but you can achieve sparkly results with a normal brush. Use short, gentle strokes, as scrubbing too hard can damage your tooth enamel and gums. Pay special attention to the area where teeth meet gums, and be sure to brush away from the gums towards the ends of your teeth. The pesky areas at the back can be fiddly to reach, so don't forget them either. Your ideal brush has soft bristles and a small enough head to reach those awkward back bits. Try to floss the gaps between your teeth after you brush as well – this will get rid of any last traces of food.

Change your toothbrush as soon as it starts to look sad and frayed, or every three months – whichever is soonest. You'll need a new one after you've been ill with a cold, too, as germs might be partying among those bristles.

No need to use 'whitening' toothpastes. These can be harsh and abrasive, scouring the surfaces of your teeth. If you're worried about the colour of your teeth, have a chat with your dentist.

Apples, raw carrots and celery sticks are smile-friendly snacks that help to clean your teeth. Fruit acids can damage your teeth's enamel, though, so best to have that apple with a piece of cheese or glass of milk (both will neutralize the acid), or drink a glass of water afterwards.

Don't compare your own, beautiful and natural smile to those of impossibly white-toothed celebrities. Most stars have had thousands of pounds' worth of dental work done, plus their photos are often digitally retouched to ramp up the whiteness. Away from Celeb-Land, teeth are rarely blindingly white. All that matters is that they're healthy, which means twice-a-day brushing for at least two minutes each time. When you drink fruit juice, brush your teeth or rinse your mouth afterwards to get rid of any acids, and go easy on the sweets, fizzy drinks and sugary snacks. Simple, huh?

How to be a gorgeous friend

Where would you be without friends? Lonely Street, that's where. They're there to share the good times and support you through life's ups and downs. And of course, whatever you get from your friends, you give right back — it's a two-way thing after all. Sometimes, though, friendships get complicated. The person you thought you knew inside out starts acting weird and distant, or maybe you just get the feeling your friendship has changed. Here's how to handle those blips.

When she seems distant and quiet ... Your first thought is probably, 'What have I done?' but try not to take her mood change personally. Sometimes, people just feel that they need a bit more space. Maybe she has things on her mind that she doesn't feel comfortable about sharing — even with you. Gently probe, maybe saying, 'You seem quiet ... is everything okay? I've just been a bit worried about you.' That way, it doesn't sound as if you're getting at her. If she says she's fine and carries on being distant, then take a deep breath and accept that that's the way things are at the moment. There's no need to drop her — you can still be your usual warm, friendly self. But it might also be a cue to widen your social circle so you're not too reliant on her.

When she's going through a tough time ... Your friend needs you more than ever — but it can be hard to know what to say or how to help. The best thing you can do is be there for her, and listen. Just being able to talk everything over will help more than you can possibly imagine — instantly, she feels less alone, and voicing problems helps to stop them blowing up out of proportion. None of this is easy. Sure, you want to help, but having problems heaped on you can be stressful for you too. So try to spent time with more upbeat friends too, just for a bit of balance (without dumping your sad friend, of course). And, if you're seriously concerned about your friend, speak to an adult you can trust. You shouldn't have to shoulder major worries alone.

When she seems to prefer another friend to you ... Think about this one carefully. Has she really dropped you in favour of someone else? Or is she the kind of girl who likes a wide social group, rather than one firm best friend? If you're not sure, just be normal and friendly with her, but in the meantime, branch out and get to know other people too. The worst thing you can do is get jealous and spiteful because she doesn't seem to have time for you. Anyway, you've got more dignity than that.

When she blabs your secret ... Not good. Maybe it popped out accidentally when she wasn't thinking. Or perhaps she's the kind of girl who can't help herself. Either way, tell her calmly that you'd trusted her to keep that secret, and think carefully before you share anything sensitive with her again.

When she brings down your mood ... Although everyone has their sad times – and of course you should support a friend when she's down – try not to hang out with people who make you feel constantly low or insecure. Sometimes people do this without meaning to – they just have a gloomy air about them, like a big black cloud. Do your best to cheer her up, but spend some time with some more positive friends too.

When she pressurizes you to do stuff you don't want to do ... Do you really want to be her friend? Trust your instincts and, if she makes you feel awkward, uncomfortable or under pressure, it's time to spread your wings. Far better to surround yourself with positive people who inspire you.

How to get your beauty sleep

It's normal to go through phases when you can't get to sleep. There you are, lying in bed with a billion thoughts zapping through your head, and the more you worry that you'll be exhausted the next day, the harder it is to drop off. There are things you can do though to prepare your body and mind for a whole night of deep, beautiful sleep. And once you've got the knack, those signs of tiredness — dark shadows under your eyes, being a bit cranky in the morning — will disappear like magic.

Try these five sleepy tricks ...

Turn off the TV. It's not a good idea to watch TV right up until you go to bed. Getting stuck into a great book is a lot more sleep-inducing — as long as the story doesn't scare your socks off, of course.

Get the temperature right. Not chilly, and not all hot and sweaty either. Some people find it easier to nod off if their bedroom window is open a chink, letting in a breath of fresh air.

Sip a warm, milky drink. Natural substances in milk can make you feel pleasantly dozy, so a hot chocolate might help you to wind down. Fizzy drinks and sweets — especially the ones stuffed with artificial colourings, sweeteners and preservatives — will keep your brain racing into the night.

Have a soothing soak. There's something about lying in a warm, sudsy bubble bath that makes you ready to curl up in your cosy bed. *Zzzz ...*

Think happy thoughts. You know what it's like — something that was only a tiny worry during the day becomes a big ball of anxiety when you start turning it over in your head at night. Instead of brooding over your worries, try to settle your mind by picturing something that makes you feel warm and happy — like a trip you went on, or a party you're going to. Then, with your eyes closed, visualize that scene in lots of detail. It'll steady your thoughts, sending you off to sleep feeling happy and at one with the world ... and the next thing you know, your mum'll be shouting that it's morning and your scrambled egg's going cold.

How to apply natural-looking make-up

You don't need to be Madonna's daughter, Lourdes, who launched her own make-up range at just 14, to be a dab hand at prettying up. Here's how to enhance your gorgeousness with just a few clever tricks.

Your gorgeous kit

- Pinky or peachy powder blusher
- Pressed powder eye shadow in your favourite shade
- Clear, brown or black mascara
- Pencil eyeliner in a shade that compliments your eye shadow (and is a teeny bit darker)
- Loose translucent powder
- Sheer or tinted lip gloss, balm or good old-fashioned Vaseline.

You'll also need

- A blusher brush
- A powder brush (looks like a bigger, fatter blusher brush)
- An eye-shadow brush or sponge-tipped applicator
- Your very own clever fingers.

It doesn't matter if you don't own all these items — the fun is in working with what you have. Remember that your brushes will need a wash in warm, soapy water from time to time though.

What to do

Tie your hair up, or clip it back, and take a good look at your face, preferable in natural daylight or a good source of light. Now check your eyebrows. Are they fairly tidy? If not, take the tiniest amount of lip balm and slick them into a neat, tidy shape, using an old, clean toothbrush if you don't have a brow brush. You'll be amazed at the difference this makes to your face.

If your face is a bit shiny — and whose isn't sometimes? — dip your brush into the translucent powder, blow off most of the particles, then sweep it lightly all over your face. It'll give a nice, even finish without having to use gunky foundation, which your young skin doesn't need. (If you really want a bit of coverage, try tinted moisturizer instead).

Brush a little eye shadow along your upper eyelids, close to your lashes. Use the smallest amount possible at first — you can always add more to build up the colour. Blend carefully so there are no hard edges.

If you want a stronger look, draw eyeliner along your upper lid, as close as you can to your upper lashes. It's easier to use lots of small, short strokes of eyeliner pencil rather than one unbroken line, which tends to wobble.

Apply a little mascara if you like (see p. 54 for some mascara tips).

Now dip your brush in your blusher, blow off most of the powder – otherwise, you'll end up with clown-like pink blobs on your cheeks. Smile, then swirl lightly over the plump parts of your cheeks. And go easy – you don't want to look over-heated.

Finally, smear on a little gloss or balm for silky-smooth lips and revel in the prettiness of you.

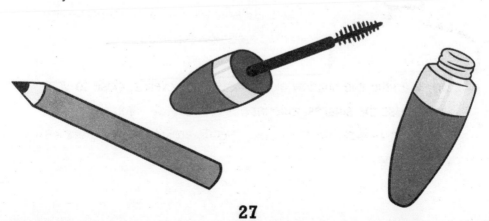

Three tips to steal

Supermodel Kate Moss reckons a little blusher makes all the difference: 'I can feel when I need it. I use a powder then a cream blush over the top.'

Kate Middleton knows the secret of lovely lips: a slightly glossy, pinky-nude lipstick (for the most natural lips, let your own lip colour be your guide).

TV presenter and style icon Alexa Chung focuses on eyes. If you want to use liquid liner like she does, apply it as close as possible to your upper lashes, finishing with a little flick at the outer corners. Practice makes perfect ...

How to cope with a blush attack

The annoying thing about blushing is that you rarely know when it's going to happen. One minute, you're normal, just getting on with your day — and the next, your whole head has turned into one huge beetroot. It happens to virtually everyone, and while there's no magic switch to turn off a blush (if only!), there are a few tricks you can try.

Breathe slowly and deeply. When you're stressed and/or embarrassed, you tend to take quick, shallow breaths. Making a conscious effort to do the opposite can bring that blush under control.

Remember it's temporary and will pass. The more you think, 'I'm blushing! I'm blushing!' the worse it feels. So try to distract yourself from those sizzling cheeks by quickly focusing your attention on something else.

Laugh it off. If someone yells, 'You've gone bright red!' just shrug, say, 'So what?' Then, as mentioned on the last page, quickly focus on something else, perhaps by asking a question about something totally unrelated ('Is that maths homework due in on Friday?'). It's amazing how a quick change of subject can turn down the heat.

Remind yourself that blushing is actually quite nice. It shows your soft, sensitive side and, if you're blushing because you've been caught doing something you shouldn't, it makes other people realize you're embarrassed and sorry. Researchers in the Netherlands have discovered that blushing actually makes people more likeable, and more likely to be forgiven!

Also ... do bear in mind that no one ever died of blushing.

How to feel gorgeous when you're tired, grumpy or upset

So you're feeling out of sorts. It's okay — none of us can be perky and sparkly all of the time. But there are things you can do to lift your mood and make you feel more relaxed and pampered — releasing your inner gorgeousness, if you like. These tips might not make the annoying or upsetting thing disappear like a popped bubble, but they will make you feel more at one with the world.

Step one ...

Move your body. Like, really move it — by going for a run or dancing until you work up a sweat. The idea is that when you exercise aerobically (which is what happens when you do continuous activities like running, swimming or cycling for at least 20 minutes), your body releases clever chemicals called endorphins. Also known as happy hormones, which perk up your mood.

Step two ...

Pamper yourself. You need private time away from everyone, so lock yourself in the bathroom for a lovely long, hot shower. Up the pamper factor by using a gentle body scrub: you can make your own in minutes by mixing a little granulated sugar and olive oil to form a gloopy paste. Massage in a light circular motion all over (apart from your face), paying extra attention to any gnarly bits like elbows or knees. Then wash off with your usual shower gel ...

31

... the sugar crystals will have gently sloughed off any rough spots, and the oil will have nourished your skin. Pat dry and slip into your cosiest PJs. Oh, and make sure you wash out the shower – all that oil's horribly slippery for the next person who goes in.

Step three ...

Laugh yourself silly. Make yourself a duvet cocoon on the sofa and stick on a comedy DVD. Laughing has been proven to make you feel better by triggering the release of endorphins (those happy hormones again). There's nothing like watching something belly-achingly funny to make those worries float away.

Three tips to steal

When Queen Cleopatra of Egypt needed to pamper, she'd soak in a bath of fresh milk. You might not fancy that – it would stink, right? – but you can make you own dairy bath soak by mixing up half a cup of whole milk powder, half a cup of oatmeal and a couple of tablespoons of honey. Spoon into a small fabric bag (or you can use a paper coffee filter, tied up with string), then tie under the hot tap so the water gushes over it, filling your bath with milky, skin-softening goodness.

Actress Zooey Deschanel loves to kick back and have fun, 'doing girlie things like dancing and singing and riding on roller coasters.' Sounds like the best cure for the blues …

Ugly Betty star America Ferrera keeps her priorities straight after a long day's filming: 'I work 14 hours in a day and then I just want to talk to my family, see the people I love, pet my dog and go to bed.'

How to make gorgeous cupcakes

Light, fluffy and deliciously sweet … how can life not feel gorgeous when you tuck into one of these?

What you need

- 115 g unsalted butter, at room temperature (slightly softened, not fridge-cold)
- 115 g caster sugar
- 115 g self-raising flour
- 2 eggs
- 2 tablespoons milk
- 1 teaspoon vanilla essence

(makes approximately 12 cupcakes).

You'll also need a 12-hole muffin tin, paper cake cases and icing sugar, plus whatever decorations you fancy – see p. 36-37 for some gorgeous suggestions.

Five steps to heaven

1. Pre-heat the oven to 180 °C, 350 °F or gas mark 4.

2. Beat the butter and sugar together with a wooden spoon until pale and fluffy, then beat in the eggs. The mixture might separate and go a bit lumpy, but that doesn't matter.

34

3. Using a sieve, sift in the flour. Carefully fold it into the mixture using a metal tablespoon, then stir in the milk and vanilla essence.

4. Spoon the mixture into the cake cases so they're around two-thirds full, then carefully put them in the oven (ask an adult to help you with this bit). Bake for around 18 minutes. Try not to keep opening the oven door for a peek as it might cause the cakes to flop (don't worry if they do, though — no one will know once they're iced).

5. Your cupcakes are ready when an inserted skewer comes out clean and not sticky. Let your cakes cool completely on a wire rack, then decorate to your heart's content. (See next page.)

Let the decorating begin!

All cupcakes are gorgeous but why not decorate them according to your mood? If you're feeling …

… girlie. Then butter-cream icing is the topping for you. Sieve 200 g icing sugar and beat in 75 g softened, unsalted butter plus a few drops of vanilla essence. Add your favourite shade of food colouring drop by drop if you like, and spread onto your cakes, using a fork for a textured effect. Or, for a truly professional finish, you can use an icing bag and pipe on the topping in impressive swirls.

… indulgent. For a rich chocolate topping add 70 g cocoa powder to your butter-cream (see above), and miss out the vanilla essence and food colouring. For a double-choc hit, grate white chocolate over your iced cakes.

… posh. Glacé icing is just right for sophisticated, grown-up-looking cakes (think posh tea party here). Beat 200 g of icing sugar with 1 tablespoon warm water and a squeeze of lemon juice, gradually adding more water (or juice) drop by drop until your icing is smooth

and spreadable. Add food colouring drop by drop too, if you like. Remember to embellish your cakes before the icing sets, otherwise your decorations might not stick.

Gorgeous decorations: silver balls * hundreds and thousands * edible glitter (in a contrasting colour to your icing) * chocolate drops * crumbled flaky chocolate (or grated chocolate) * halved strawberries, fresh raspberries or blueberries * mini marshmallows * your friends' names written in icing pen (or even mini portraits of them if you're feeling ambitious) * jellybeans or Smarties * sugar flowers * mini chocolate eggs * birthday-cake candles.

How to de-clutter your bedroom

Ah, your own private space. Your little corner of the world where you can hang out with friends, listen to music, tackle your homework without distractions and generally do your own thing. But what if it's not the kind of place you want to be? If it's jam-packed with tatty old games, soft toys with their stuffing hanging out and ancient clothes that haven't fitted you since you were six? All this clutter is officially **Not Gorgeous**, and here's why:

• Too much stuff means you can never find the things you really like, and waste precious time searching.

• It creates an atmosphere of confusion and can bring down your mood.

• On top of all that, your mum's always on at you to tidy it up.

So how to bust that clutter? First up, decide on three 'sorting categories' along these lines …

Love: The things you want to have out on display or close to hand – your favourite, or most useful possessions, for instance.

Need: Other stuff you like and use, but which can be stored away until you need it.

Dump: The stuff you've outgrown, don't like or never use any more, which is just cluttering up your life. You can divide this into two sub-categories:

Dump in the bin (for anything that's really wrecked) and

Charity Shop **Dump** for items in good condition.

— — Take a deep breath and get started … — — — — — — —

Okay, here's the tough part. Don't make the mistake of dragging out everything into a massive pile or you'll just stare at it and want to run away. Tackle just one small area at a time — like your wardrobe, a shelf or a chest of drawers. That's quite enough for one de-cluttering session.

If the '**Need**' stuff won't fit neatly away, think about getting some clear plastic boxes with lids to slide under your bed, which can hold a huge amount of stuff. Oh, and don't forget to reward yourself when you're done!

So there you have it …

… a calm and clutter-free room, which, even if it's pretty tiny, will suddenly seem so much bigger. Now you can take a good look at your space and decide how to display your favourite things, and maybe even think about a new colour scheme. When you've made a mammoth effort to de-clutter and tidy, parents can often become keener to get out the paint roller.

How to choose what to use on your hair

The right hair product can tackle all kinds of problems (although not maths ones, unfortunately) and transform your style. Don't worry – you won't need a great stash of bottles and pots. Just find the one you like, perhaps trying a mini size first, and treat it as your hair's best friend.

To add volume ...

Styling mousse couldn't be easier to use. Just work a golf-ball-sized blob through damp hair before styling – it'll make it feel thicker, more manageable and is especially good on fine, flyaway tresses. Spray wax adds volume too, and is especially good for a slightly messy, tousled look. It can also be used to define curls.

To add texture ...

Texturizers are for giving your hair, well ... texture, and they work best on short hair. There are tons of types – wax, clay, putty and, confusingly, gel-wax. Although they all do a similar job, some are stickier and heavier than others. While clay tends to give a matt effect, wax can also add shine – it's a just a matter of finding a type you like.

To use, rub a dab of product between your fingers to warm and soften it (go easy – you don't want to put on too much) and work through damp or dry hair until it's as rough and choppy-looking as you like. If you prefer a sleeker style, just work in a tiny amount and comb through. These products can build up in the hair, making it dull, so it's important to shampoo it all out. With the really waxy types, you might need to use a little neat shampoo without water first, then shampoo out as normal.

To de-frizz ...

Leave-in conditioner is combed through your hair after washing (towel-dry your hair first so it's just moist, not drippy). As the name suggests, you don't wash it out. Before styling, you can also work through a little serum to smooth those frizzy bits — again, a teeny amount goes a long way. Or try a styling cream: as well as taming frizz, it should boost shine too. If your problem's more wild, tangly locks, a spritz of detangling spray on damp hair should persuade it to behave.

To add shine ...

Use styling cream, as above, or spray shine (sometimes called glossing mist) as a finishing touch after styling.

To protect ...

If you use straighteners or any other heated appliances, a protective spray or lotion will help to stop your hair drying out. Basically, you're forming a barrier so your hair doesn't sizzle (see p. 163).

To hold a style ...

Hairspray's what you need. Just a quick squirt, though — you don't want your hair to look (and feel) stiff and meringue-like.

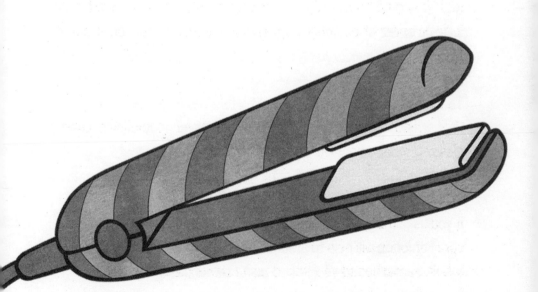

How to make nervousness work for you

No one feels 100% confident all of the time. Occasionally, an attack of the terrors comes on, sometimes when you least expect it. Nerves can be good thing though. Not when it's to the point where you're trembling and can barely speak, but that slightly hyped-up nervousness that sharpens all your senses can really be a good thing. So, if you're prone to the jitters, here's what to do ...

1. Prepare, prepare, prepare. Before anything scary, make sure you're completely ready for it and well rested. When you're winging it and don't really know what you're doing, nervousness can spiral out of control.

2. Don't let nervousness freak you out. Instead, regard it as a good thing that makes you feel completely engaged with what you're about to do (it's the opposite of that half-hearted 'So what?' sort of feeling, which can make you feel a bit flat). As Beyoncé says: 'I get nervous when I don't get nervous. If I'm nervous I know I'm going to have a good show.' Actress Emma Watson agrees that it's good to be a just a little scared: 'I think it's important to have that extra adrenaline. It gives you that extra zing.'

3. Remember it'll all be over in a jiffy. To knock your fears down to size, remind yourself (or find out) how long the nerve-wracking thing will last. For instance, if it's a music exam, keep telling yourself it'll only be 20 minutes and of course you can handle that. Imagine yourself after the event, feeling confident, proud and doing something nice and relaxing with a big smile on your face.

4. Take a moment to breathe. If your nervousness is in danger of tipping into sheer terror, try breathing slowly and deeply to steady yourself, and take a few moments' time-out to be by yourself. Sipping water, and holding your wrists under a cool running tap can help too.

5. Remember they're just ordinary people. If you have to face an audience, an examiner or someone you find intimidating, then imagine them doing something really ordinary like picking their nose or sitting on the loo.

6. Above all, be brave and believe in yourself. As JK Rowling says: 'Anything's possible if you've got enough nerve.' And she should know …

How to have gorgeous nails

For such tiny things, nails can have a big impact. Treat them to a manicure and you'll instantly feel smarter and more 'finished'. Here's how.

1. The tidying bit. Pushing back your cuticles (the part where the base of your nail meets the skin) makes things look neater. But go really gently – it's a delicate area and the cuticle does a fine job of protecting the new nail as it grows. It can become sore or even infected if you hack away at it willy-nilly. To avoid damage, carefully ease it back with a wooden stick that's specially shaped for the job. If you do this during or just after a bath, your skin will be softer. Massaging hand cream into your cuticles will also soften them up.

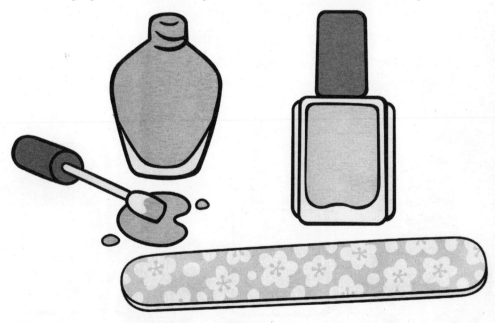

2. The shaping bit. Using an emery board, file your nails into the shape you want (shortish ovals are the most practical and prettiest). File in one direction only, from side to tip, as back-and-forth sawing can weaken and damage the nail.

3. The shining bit. For a natural healthy shine, a buffer block is fabulous piece of kit. You just rub lightly but briskly over the nail for a brilliant, long-lasting shine. The beauty of buffing is there's no polish to chip or retouch. It's almost magical, how glassy-smooth your nails look after a good buff.

4. The colouring bit. If you're in the mood for colour, it's worth taking the trouble to apply a clear base coat first. This'll make your polish last longer and prevents deep shades from staining your nails. Once it's dry, try to apply your colour in just three strokes — one up each side of the nail, followed by one up the middle. Allow them to dry thoroughly, then apply a second coat (this will make your colour

last longer). To be truly professional, wait for the second coat to dry and apply clear polish on top to seal in that delicious colour.

Special effects
The sky's the limit when it comes to customizing your nails ...

French polish ... très chic, and easy if you have a steady hand. Paint your nails in a sheer pale pink polish, then, when it's dry, apply white polish to the tips only.

Sparkle and shine ... glittery polish looks great on its own, but is even better layered over a deep, dramatic colour like black, violet or navy.

Doodle tips ... nail pens have tiny tips so you can design and draw to your heart's content. Tiny polka dots are a good starting point.

Nail nasties (and how to banish them)

Bitten nails ... You might bite your nails when you're worried or bored – or perhaps it's just a habit you don't know how to break. Foul-tasting anti-biting lotions can work (just paint them on like nail polish). Chewing gum can help too – if your mouth's busily gnawing away, you're less likely to nibble anything else. Bear in mind that nails only grow at around 2.5 millimetres a month – so if yours are all bitten away, that's a long time to wait for nice, healthy new ones!

White spots on nails ... These can be caused by a zinc deficiency (zinc is a mineral found in meat or fish – if you're veggie, a vitamin supplement containing zinc might help). Sometimes, the spots might be the result of a bump to the nail, and will just grow out naturally.

Weak nails that split and break ... Buffing too often (or too vigorously) can be the culprit here, so limit yourself to no more than once a week. Your diet might also be low on the vitamins and minerals that nails love. Tuck into plenty of fresh fruit, veg, fish, meat, eggs and cheese – it'll help to keep your hair glossy and lustrous too (as hair and nails are made up from pretty much the same thing).

How to draw gorgeous illustrations

Maybe you're a brilliant artist, or perhaps you think you're not so creative — either way, anyone can draw because what makes a gorgeous illustration is your own personal style. Here's how to discover yours.

Finding that style requires some uninterrupted time with no one poking their nose in (because having people peer at your work-in-progress can make you feel self-conscious). So get comfortable in your bedroom and politely shut the door.

Gather together all the art materials you can find. You might have pencils, charcoal, roller pens, felt tips, maybe a fine brush and ink — even the stubby crayons from when you were little. Try hard and soft pencils ('B' pencils are soft, 'H' are hard — ones marked 'HB' are in the middle). Get everything out, plus a sketch pad. It needn't be posh — in fact, really fancy expensive ones can be a bit intimidating.

Now, rather than being told what to draw like you might be at school, take a moment to think about the kind of illustration you'd like to create. Maybe it'll be a series of fashion illustrations or a graphic novel-style short story told in comic-strip frames. It might be a scene you've dreamed up in your head, or a personalized birthday card for your best friend.

Still stuck? Have a flick through any illustrated books you have on your shelves to glean some ideas. Look at which illustrations grab your eye and have a go at a similar style. If you still have old picture books from when you were little, look at them too. Illustrations can be any style – you only have to compare the *Wimpy Kid* books, with their funny little stick boys, to the beautiful retro-style drawings in Madonna's *The English Roses*, to see that anything goes.

Don't feel bad about copying (look upon it as being inspired instead). Every artist in the world has been influenced by artists who've gone before. When an artist copies another person's work, they usually sign it with their own name, then add 'after Picasso' (or whoever the artist is).

Still hesitant? Then start doodling and see where it takes you.

Why drawing is a gorgeous thing to do: doing something creative gives you a good feeling * the more you draw, the better an artist you'll be – it's all about practice * you can cut out your beautiful drawings and make them into gift tags or cards * it's a private thing – you can do it without anyone else butting in or expressing an opinion * doodling has been proven to be hugely relaxing and helps to ease those worries away.

Flowers Floral doodles show that you're feeling wistful, thoughtful and appreciate beautiful things.

Faces Happy expressions mean you're sunny and good-natured, while beautiful faces suggest that this is how you want to appear to the world.

Animals Cute creatures reveal your fun, playful and caring side.

Spiky designs These suggest that you're feeling angry and frustrated.

Hearts You're optimistic, love life and really value your friends.

Stars These little sparkles show an ambitious streak and suggest you'll go far.

Houses You're feeling happy, cosy and content with your life.

Random swirls You're happy, relaxed and always fun to be around — a real party girl.

How to have gorgeous eyelashes

Celebrities' lashes tend to be long, lush and cheek-grazing. They can also look a bit fake (because, of course, they are fake). In real life — not on Planet Celeb — natural lashes are a whole lot nicer. That's not to say you can't treat yours to a lick of mascara if you feel like it. But the effect to go for is a slight enhancement — not full-on fakery. Here's how ...

Unless your hair's very dark, in which case black mascara is fine, brown mascara looks more natural. Clear mascara is great too. It makes lashes glossy, so they appear thicker, without adding colour.

Mascara can easily look blobby and clumpy, so lightly wipe the wand onto a tissue before applying, so your lashes just get a light coating.

Start with your upper lashes, first looking down and stroking the wand downwards. They open your eyes wide, look up and brush upwards to give your lashes a bit of a curl. Gently wipe the wand clean-ish and brush through again if there are any blobby bits. You can also add mascara to your lower lashes, although there's probably no need — the colour and curl of your upper lashes will give you enough impact.

To avoid waking up with panda eyes and a smeared pillow, make sure you remove all of your make-up before bed (mascara especially needs make-up remover to shift it). Add a little to a cotton pad, look down and sweep the pad downwards over your eyes.

Don't bother with waterproof mascara unless you really need it — it's harder to remove at the end of the day.

Ancient mascara can cause watery eyes and irritation, so if yours has been hanging around for a year or more, treat yourself to a new one (out of all the types of make-up, mascara has the shortest shelf life and can make eyes itchy and irritable if it's old).

For extra impact, try using eyelash curlers: just squeeze gently for a few seconds. Top make-up artist Bobbi Brown advises: 'If you choose to curl your lashes, be sure to do this before applying mascara.' Curling after mascara can make those delicate lashes more prone to breaking.

How to make a gorgeous lip balm

Making your own lip balm couldn't be easier. You will need to buy a couple of simple ingredients (shea butter and beeswax), but they're not too expensive and easy to order online. Plus, once you have them, you'll be able to make lots of gorgeously scented and packaged balms to give to your friends.

What you need

- 30 g olive oil
- 10 g shea butter
- 10 g beeswax
- A tiny drop of perfumed oil (optional)

- Four or five tiny containers for your lip balms such as mini jam jars, or empty plastic pots from old lip glosses or eye creams (ask your mum to save hers). You might also find cute retro eye-shadow and lip-gloss compacts in charity shops
- Sticky labels to decorate.

What to do

In a heavy-based saucepan, gently heat the olive oil, shea butter and beeswax, adding the perfumed oil if you're using any. Shea butter and beeswax melt quickly and easily, so don't let your mixture get too hot – gentle warming is what's needed. All you do now is fill your containers carefully and leave to cool overnight. Slick on for the softest lips ever. Was there ever a more thoughtful, personal gift?

How to pack a gorgeous lunchbox

Your mum or dad might still pack your lunchbox, and they probably try their best, but sometimes — well, quite often — it's just not ... gorgeous. There'll be a sandwich in there, maybe some crisps, and a piece of fruit that you might bring back home a little dented and looking sorry for itself. This kind of lunch will banish hunger pangs, but hardly sets your taste buds alight.

So imagine a packed lunch that's jam-packed with nutrients, filling you up without making you sleepy, and being good for you while still tasting fantastic. It might take a little longer, but, if you're organized, you can put much of it together the night before and store it in the fridge. The ideal lunch consists of four different sections: carbohydrates, protein, fruit and/or a vegetable, and something ... treaty. Choose something yummy from each section and know you're getting everything your body needs.

The carb bit. Carbohydrates are vital for energy. While sugary cookies and cakes give that energy boost, it's short-lived and can make you feel tired and sluggish later. The best kind of carbs release energy slowly, so you're perky right through the afternoon. Try one of these:

• A wholemeal roll, baguette, wrap, chapatti or bagel (see? lunch need never be boring) filled with lean ham or chicken, crunchy salad and a small dollop of mayonnaise. Tuna mixed with sweetcorn and mayo is another great choice, as this fishy friend is thought to help concentration.

• A small pot of couscous, pasta, rice or noodle salad.

The protein bit. This is essential for the body's growth and repair, and great for skin and hair too. Your sandwich filling will provide some protein, but an extra bit never hurt anyone. Choose from:

• An individually wrapped cheese portion (great to up your calcium quota).

• A chicken drumstick with foil wrapped around the bone so you don't get greasy fingers.

• A foil parcel of ham or salami.

The vitamin-packed bit. These feel so fresh, you know they're doing you good. Try one of these:

• A small pot of thin carrot sticks, red pepper or cucumber make a crunchy lunch – pop in some cherry tomatoes too.

• Any fruit you fancy, from a humble apple (great for slow-release energy), pear or tangerine to a slice of watermelon or a halved kiwi to eat with a teaspoon. Bananas don't travel so well, unless you have one of those plastic 'banana guard' containers to keep it bash-free. Grapes and berries are best packed in a small plastic tub, and you can make your own mini fruit salad too.

• A small box of raisins, a few dried apricots or banana chips.

The treat bit. Because you deserve it – the clever thing is, these are good for you too:

• Yogurt, fromage frais or fruit jelly.

• A crunchy, chocolate-y cereal bar.

• Homemade popcorn with a little salt or sugar added.

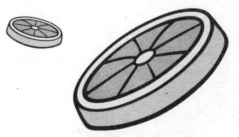

Remember something to drink ... as staying hydrated boosts your brainpower throughout the day.

• Store your mini fruit juice cartons in the freezer. In the morning, pop a frozen carton in your lunchbox — it'll have defrosted, but still be lovely and cool, by lunchtime.

• Chocolate milk might be a bit of a treat but it's also calcium-packed, so great for bones and teeth.

• Water is the best thing to sip during the day, so slip a bottle in your school bag in addition to your lunchtime drink, or befriend the school water cooler.

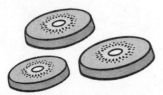

Hate meat and fish? Love cheese?

Here are four protein-packed cheesy sandwich fillings to try.

Cheese and apple. Grate some cheddar, peel an apple and grate that too. Add a finely chopped spring onion and a little mayonnaise, plus a squeeze of lemon juice.

Cheese and coleslaw. Add thin slices of your favourite cheese, then a thin layer of coleslaw and finally some crispy lettuce (which will stop the bread going soggy). Or grate your cheese, mix with coleslaw and use to fill your sarnie.

Cheesy banana. This one's delicious on granary bread. Spread with cream cheese, then add thin slices of banana (a squirt of lemon juice will stop them going brown) and a tiny dribble of honey.

Cheese and pickle. Not forgetting, of course, grated cheddar with a thin layer of pickle. Heaven.

How to give yourself (or a lucky friend) a gorgeous pedicure

Poor feet. They spend most of their time stuffed into tights, socks and shoes, all neglected. Treating yourself to a pedicure is well worth the effort — the results are amazing, and it's relaxing, too. From plain and unloved to pampered and pretty — don't your feet deserve it?

Remove any old polish then use clippers to trim your nails. Cut them straight across, as curved nails can grow into the skin and be … ouch! … quite painful.

Now file your nails, using an emery board, to smooth away any rough bits.

Massage a hand cream or foot cream all over your feet to make them baby-soft. Nail polish doesn't stick well to greasy nails, so wipe them with a flannel or cotton-wool pad dipped in a little soapy water. Pat your nails dry.

At this stage you can use toe separators if you have them — these are spongy devices that fit between your toes to keep them splayed out, so polish is less likely to smudge. If you don't have any, you can separate your toes with tissue.

Now for the creative part. To make your colour last, apply a clear base coat and let it dry before brushing on two coats of colour. Finish with a coat of clear polish to seal in the colour.

Admire your gorgeous tootsies!

How to handle a confidence wobble

Everyone has these from time to time. It can happen when a friend looks truly amazing, when you're all casual and didn't wash your hair that day. Or when you open a magazine or look at a website and there's some incredibly beautiful celebrity gazing back at you. Whenever you're overcome by a wobble, try to think one of these positive thoughts ...

For friend envy

My friend looks lovely but so do I, in a different way. She has off days too, just like I do. Her life isn't perfect because no one's is. There are things about me that are unique to me.

For those 'no one likes me' moments

I don't have to be the most popular girl in my class or friendship group to be liked and appreciated. I don't have to be the loudest or most obviously confident either. I just have to be me.

For those 'I'll never look as good as people on TV' wobbles

So what? They've been made up and blow-dried to within an inch of their lives. Veteran supermodel Cindy Crawford once admitted: 'Even I don't look like Cindy Crawford.' In magazines and on huge billboard adverts, even more trickery is at work: these girls have been digitally retouched. Not just to erase the odd pimple or eye bag, but almost completely redrawn, like airbrushed Barbies. These images **aren't real**.

When someone says something mean

People usually say mean things because they want a reaction, as it makes them feel more important. It gains them attention, too – it's a way of saying, 'Notice me!' Which is pretty sad really.

When someone laughs at you

Who cares? Sometimes I think I'm funny too. And I'm strong and secure enough to be able to laugh at myself.

For that 'help – I'm doing a test and my mind's gone blank' wobble

It's just nerves that are making my mind seize up. If I breathe slowly and deeply and carry on with the questions I can answer, I'll feel calmer and can go back to the tricky ones later. If I work steadily and thoughtfully, I'll be gaining points all along the way.

Three tips to steal

Don't think small, think big! Actress Chloë Moretz believes in having firm ambitions: 'I'd love to write, direct and produce my own movies. I'm an overachiever, you know?'

Although actress Audrey Hepburn was one of Hollywood's most gorgeous stars ever, she believed that confidence is more powerful than beauty alone. So, when you're feeling wobbly, repeat her mantra: 'Nothing is impossible. The world itself says I'm possible.'

Selena Gomez reckons you should never compare yourself to anyone else: 'Always be true to yourself,' she says. 'There's no one better!'

What kind of gorgeous are you?

Everyone has their own kind of gorgeousness, so what's yours? Try this quiz to find out. Make a note of your answers as you go along.

1. How do you go about packing your holiday suitcase?

a) I throw in tons of tops, shorts and trainers — it takes minutes
b) I bundle in all my favourite, quirky bits and pieces (I'll figure out how to wear them when I get there)
c) Outfits are laid out on my bed before I pack
d) I just pack the favourites I wear all the time, plus a couple of dressy things

2. Do you have someone you look to for style inspiration?

a) I like to see what celebs are wearing, but tend to stick to what suits me
b) No — I follow my instincts and create my own look
c) Yes — I'm always poring over magazines
d) Not at all — I just dress for whatever I'm doing that day

3. What's the worst thing anyone could force you to wear?

a) Anything ugly and old-fashioned
b) A cutting-edge look from the catwalk that I can't carry off

c) Fussy, flouncy clothes that stop me doing what I want

d) The boring current 'look' that everyone else is wearing

4. How do you choose your accessories?

a) They're carefully thought out to finish my look

b) I don't really wear them – too fussy

c) I might add something just to perk up a fairly plain outfit

d) I grab whatever I feel like on the day – the more the better!

5. How long does it take to get dressed on a (non-school) morning?

a) If I've got plenty of time, I take ages trying things on and experimenting

b) Minutes – I just pull on what's practical for the day ahead

c) I tend to wear similar things so it's easy and quick

d) I like to take my time so I look just right

6. How do you decide on which haircut to have?

a) It needs to be short and simple or long enough to tie back

b) I'll check out the magazines and choose my favourite look

c) I'm always chopping and changing so I tend to just go with my mood on the day

d) I'll usually go for the tried-and-tested style that suits me

7. How do your friends react to your personal style?

a) They seem to like it — well, they're always asking to borrow things!

b) They laugh at me sometimes, but I think they quite like it

c) We don't really talk about — it's just who I am

d) Occasionally they suggest I should be a bit more adventurous

8. What do you do with your old clothes that have gone out of style?

a) I keep them — they're handy for a dress-down, messing-about sort of day

b) They tend to be completely worn out so it's the bin, I'm afraid

c) I'll pass them on to friends or charity

d) I hang onto them in case I can customize or update them, or wear them in a new way

9. Your friend decides to give you a complete make-over. How do you feel about the experience?

a) I'm amazed by the results. It's so rare that I'm all done up

b) It's fun, and fascinating to see how someone else views me

c) A bit uncomfortable, as I know how I like to look

d) I enjoy it — but am just as happy to get back to the real me!

10. What's your dream job?

a) Something creative like an artist or designer
b) A top sportswoman
c) I'd love to work in the fashion industry – like a photographer, model or fashion editor
d) Anything that play to my strengths – like a scientist or musician

So what's your kind of gorgeous?

Figure out your score and find out …

1. a) 0, b) 1, c) 2, d) 3   **6.** a) 0, b) 2, c) 1, d) 3
2. a) 3, b) 1, c) 2, d) 0   **7.** a) 2, b) 1, c) 0, d) 3
3. a) 2, b) 3, c) 0, d) 1   **8.** a) 3, b) 0, c) 2, d) 1
4. a) 2, b) 0, c) 3, d) 1   **9.** a) 0, b) 1, c) 2, d) 3
5. a) 1, b) 0, c) 3, d) 2   **10.** a) 1, b) 0, c) 2, d) 3

If you scored 0-7 ... you're gorgeously sporty

With your active lifestyle you don't spend too much time worrying about your appearance — there are far better things to do. Where hair and clothes are concerned, the simpler the better: you need to be good to go in a matter of minutes, so why make things more complicated? You rarely bother with make-up and look great as you are — all fresh, glowing skin and glossy hair that other girls would die for. With your sunny nature and positive attitude to life, you make other people's lives a little more gorgeous too.

Your gorgeous must-haves:
trusty trainers * stretchy tops and shorts * hair bands * lip balm.

If you scored 8-15 ... you're gorgeously quirky

You're the most individual girl in your friendship group, always thinking of new ways to create a look. While you love fashion, you're far too imaginative to slavishly follow a style — anyway, you don't want to look like anyone else. What's so clever about your sense of style is that it looks effortless, as if you've just thrown it together — yet somehow, you manage to look amazing. Whether you plunder the sale rail or discover a vintage treasure, one thing's for sure: your look will always be unique.

Your gorgeous must-haves: unusual jewellery * opaque tights in many colours * vintage tops, skirts and bags * lots of eye shadow shades to experiment with.

If you scored 16-23 ... you're gorgeously stylish

You love fashion and keep a close eye on trends, yet have a knack for picking the ones that suit you. Although you're sometimes inspired by a celebrity's fashion choices, you're just as likely to glean inspiration as you flick through the fashion pages of your favourite magazines. Sometimes, you'll update your look with a new piece of jewellery, a scarf or belt: you're an expert on staying on-trend without spending a fortune, and know those little touches count for a lot. Friends often ask for your opinion on a look, knowing you'll give great advice, as you always look amazing. Lucky you!

Your gorgeous must-haves: fashion mags to browse * a great pair of jeans to dress up or down * a stylish jacket * the right bag to finish your look.

If you scored 24-30 ... you're gorgeously natural

Getting dressed in the morning couldn't be easier — you know what suits you and have favourites you turn to time and time again. That doesn't mean your style's boring — more that you've discovered what works with your colouring and lifestyle, so you instinctively know what's going to look great. The result? You've evolved your own, personal, easy-going look. There are no early-morning style panics, and rarely a fashion disaster either. You always look utterly relaxed, stylish and happy in your own skin, and never as if you've tried too hard.

Your gorgeous must-haves: a much-loved sweater * favourite jeans * beloved boots and ballet flats * a hint of lip gloss.

73

How to keep your gorgeous memories safe

It's so easy to forget about special times, so why not create a memory box to store all those little things that are special to you?

Start by finding a box – one roughly the size of a shoebox is ideal. You can buy a posh one or decorate and customize a plain one to make it your own.

Tape an envelope to the inside (perhaps under the lid) to store photos and small paper items.

Now gather together all the things that'll trigger memories in years to come. They might be special photos, birthday cards or messages from friends, or tickets or wristbands from gigs, festivals or events you've been to. You might also add a friendship bracelet given by someone special, a sugar wrapper from a favourite holiday café, or a tiny toy from your past.

Be selective – a small collection of special photos is better than a huge pile. You can store the rest of your photos somewhere else – a memory box is really for treasured items only.

You might want to add a tiny label or message to certain items to remind you why they're special, or about the story that's attached to them.

Once you've started your memory box, look out for more bits and pieces to put in it. The great thing is that it keeps evolving and growing as time goes on.

Keep it somewhere safe, and bring it out whenever you feel nostalgic and want to look back upon happy times.

A memory box is the story of you
Peek inside when you feel blue
(Or even when you don't!)

How to have gorgeous skin

Skincare can seem horribly complicated, with a dizzying amount of products to choose from. The good news, though, is that your young skin doesn't need to be loaded with creams and potions. It's just a matter of keeping it lovely and clean, and moisturising if it's feeling dry. Here's all you need to be peachy.

Rise and shine: your morning routine

Cleanse. There are tons of cleansers and facial washes available, from the kind you wipe away with cotton wool or wash straight off with water. Some are creamy, some foamy, others more of a gel-type. A wash-off cleanser or facial wash is probably best as they whisk away grime in an instant. When you find a brand that suits you – one that doesn't leave your skin feeling dry, tight or cause a break-out – stick to it like your new best friend. No point in trying a wide range of washes just for the sake of it.

'What's wrong with soap?' you might ask. While it does shift the grime, it can be horribly drying and isn't as kind to your skin as a specially formulated cleanser or facial wash. Facial wipes are fine too, as long as you splash on water on afterwards to remove any traces of fluid.

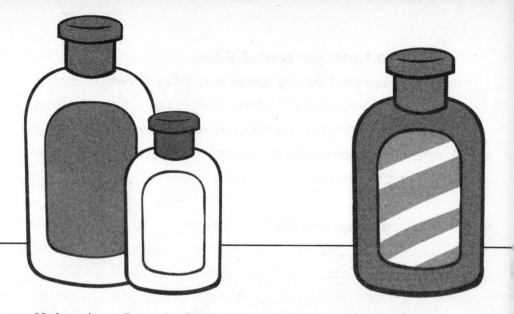

Moisturize. (But only if you need it.) After cleansing, you might be good to go. In which case, just gently pat your skin dry and get on with your day. However, you might feel your skin needs a drop of moisturizer to keep it super-soft. Choose a light, unperfumed lotion type and massage in the tiniest amount. Remember: you only need moisturizer if your skin's dry, flaky or rough — otherwise leave it be.

Good night, gorgeous: your sleepy-time steps

Cleanse again. Yep — even if bed is calling you, as your skin won't thank you for leaving it clogged with the day's grime. If you're wearing make-up, cleansing will probably be enough to sweep that away too, but you might also need a make-up remover to get rid of the last traces.

Moisturize. (Again, only if your skin's crying out for a drink.) You won't need night cream as these are for older skins.

Treat. Dab any blemishes with spot stick to encourage them to heal while you sleep (there's more info on spots and blemishes on p. 105-107).

Which skin type are you?

Normal skin is neither oily nor dry — it's somewhere in between. Pretty perfect, really — lucky girl.

Oily skin often looks shiny and feels greasy to the touch, especially around the nose, forehead and chin (where there are more oil-producing glands). You might be more prone to spots and blackheads too. While it's important to cleanse, don't use anything too harsh or oil-stripping, as it'll cause your skin to produce even more oil, almost in revenge.

Dry skin can feel tight and sort of papery, and is prone to flaky or pinkish patches. It can become even dryer in the winter, when the central heating's on and humidity is low outside (there's less moisture in the air). Hot summer days, and being in the sea and swimming pool, can be drying too. A light moisturizer will keep it soft and supple.

Combination skin means both dry and oily. Certain areas (usually your nose, forehead and chin) are usually oily, while other parts, such as your cheeks, tend to be dry. Thoroughly cleanse all of your face, and soothe the dry bits with moisturizer.

Sensitive skin (which tends to be dry too) reacts easily to changes in skincare and the weather, flaring up in pink patches and rashes. It might be itchy too. Use the gentlest products you can find, and if anything upsets your skin, stop using it right away.

Other ways to love your skin

Sleep on it ... Not enough sleep means sallow skin and dark circles under the eyes. Good enough reason to get plenty of sleep!

Glug-glug-glug ... No need to drink so much water that you're constantly dashing to the loo. Make sure you're hydrated throughout the day, though. Water really is the best liquid fuel for your body.

Get moving ... Exercise boosts circulation, making your whole body function more effectively. Fresh air gives you a glow too.

Vitamins 'r' us ... While eating fresh, nutritious foods can't magic away spots, it will help to keep your skin clear (sweets, cakes and fried foods are fine as occasional treats, of course). Think of a healthy diet as skincare from the inside.

How to take gorgeous photos

There are no real rules about photography. It's all about getting to know your camera (or camera-phone) and experimenting. So, rather than lots of dos and don'ts, here are a few suggestions to unleash your imagination ...

Get to know your camera and its different modes. You might be impatient to get shooting but it's worth trying out all the different settings first.

Try different angles. This often makes a so-so picture stunning. Try shooting from above, low down or a side view. When you start to move around your subject (the person or object you're photographing), your images will become more interesting.

Check your background. Obviously, you want to avoid objects that look like they're growing out of your subject's head. Fussy backgrounds can be distracting but, if you photograph a friend standing against, say, a graffitied wall, it can look great. Experiment with different backgrounds, moving your subject around if you can (er, not if it's a building, obviously).

Try going really, really close. The most powerful images are often close up.

Get inspired. Magazines and big coffee table books are often filled with stunning photography. Have a look through some and see if they spark any ideas.

Avoid flash if you possibly can. It's not terribly kind to faces and can create harsh shadows. Natural daylight is softer and more flattering.

Keep your horizon horizontal. If it's wonky and sloping, your picture will have a strange, sea-sicky effect.

Keep your eyes open and your camera with you. All kinds of subjects make great photos – not just people but the things you see every day in your neighbourhood and even your own home. Snap away and create a visual diary of your life.

How to choose gorgeous eye-shadow shades

Playing around with eye shadow is one of the most fun things about make-up. There aren't any fixed rules, but you might want to try contrasting your eye shadow to your own eye colour. That way, it'll really bring out and intensify the colour of your eyes — stunning! So if your eyes are ...

... blue. Try an earthy-brown palette — anything from creamy pale shades to deep chocolate.

... brown. Almost any colour works well with your eyes. Try all shades of blue, from lighter, sparkly colours to striking deep navy. Warm, rusty colours work well too.

... green. Purplish shades such as lilac, plum and violet draw attention to green eyes. For a more natural look, brownish colours work wonderfully too.

... grey. Shades of purple, brown and even metallic coppery shades look stunning against your unusual eye colour.

... hazel. Like green eyes, purplish colours can bring out your gorgeous colour — try warm russets and brownish shades too.

What about super-bright eye shadows?

These guidelines don't mean you shouldn't play around with zingy colours like hot pinks, yellows, greens and even oranges. They're just a little trickier to get right, so start by applying a neutral colour like beige over your eyelid, then add a hint of brighter colour. It's best to build up a sizzling shade bit by bit, rather than brushing on loads and having to tone it down because it looks scary.

How to make a gorgeous bath melt

Dropping a bath melt into warm water won't produces mounds of frothy bubbles, but it is a great way to soothe and soften while you soak. They also make gorgeous presents, packaged in boxes and nestling in scrunched-up tissue paper. Make sure you mark them 'NOT TO BE EATEN' though, as they really do look scrumptious!

What you need

- 200 g cocoa butter (this can be ordered easily online)
- 100 g oil such as almond oil or any body oil
- A few drops of perfumed oil
- Mini cupcake cases (the ones that are used for truffles – normal-sized ones are too big)
- Decorations such as dried petals, flowers and a little glitter (the very fine, edible kind, used for sprinkling on cakes, is ideal).

What to do

1. Gently melt the cocoa butter in a heavy-based pan. The butter melts very easily, so keep the heat down low — it shouldn't get too hot, but do be careful. Turn off the heat as soon as it's liquefied.

2. Stir in the oils and carefully pour into your paper cases.

3. Sprinkle on your decorations before they've set, or they won't stick to the bath melts.

4. Leave in a cool place to set overnight. Popping them in the fridge for an hour or so will firm them up and make it easier to peel off the paper cases (or you can leave them in their cases if you prefer).

How to be a gorgeous daughter (and sister)

Families. Even though you love yours to bits, parents and siblings can sometimes drive you **mad**. The fact is they're there, under your feet, borrowing your stuff and telling you what to do. Next time you feel as if you're about to blow a fuse, try one of these calming strategies instead …

'My little sister/brother keeps pestering me.' Ah, the perils of younger siblings. For such small people, they can create a heck of a lot of noise, mess and fuss. First, think about your friends' little siblings: chances are they're just as annoying, so you're not alone. It's also completely normal — that's the way most small kids are.

If you can bear it, try to give them a little time and attention, because that's what they crave. Reading a story or playing a game might be enough to satisfy them, then they'll go off and do something else. Constantly telling them to go away will only make them more hell-bent on grabbing your attention, so then you're back to square one. Also, being a kind big sis will give you a (well-deserved) feeling of pride and all-round goodness. You'll gain Brownie points from your parents too.

'Mum won't let me go on a sleepover.' Rotten one, this, especially if everyone else is allowed to go. Here's what doesn't help: sulking, raging and slamming doors. It's far better to talk to your mum about why she's saying no (if she hasn't told you already), then you can put your case forward in a mature, thoughtful way.

For instance, is she worried because she doesn't know the parents? Fair enough – no caring mum would let her daughter stay overnight at a stranger's house. Perhaps they can meet, or at the very least have a chat on the phone. Or could the sleepover switch to the house of someone she does know? Without nagging and moaning (which will only put her back up), try to think your way around the problem. And remember that she cares about you and isn't deliberately trying to spoil your fun.

'I feel like I can't do anything right.' Take some time to figure out if that's really the case. If you feel you're being unfairly treated, choose a calm moment (not in the middle of an argument) to explain your point of view. Hopefully, that way you'll be listened to. But be honest with yourself too. If you have done something wrong, it's always best to apologize, as it shows you're grown-up enough to admit when you're wrong. Most parents' hearts melt when someone says sorry in a genuine way.

'My big sister/brother picks on me.' No one should be bullied or humiliated – and that means at home too. If your sister or brother is annoying you, be specific about their behaviour and tell them you want it to stop. Saying, 'I don't want you to make fun of me in front of my friends is better than a vague, 'You're horrible.' If you feel like you're not getting anywhere, speak to another family member who can have a word on your behalf.

'Everyone steals my stuff.' Quite simply, ask them not to. To show how reasonable you are, you could tell them what you don't mind lending – as long as they ask first. If something's really precious to you, store it away in a secret hiding place instead of leaving it sitting on your desk, all tempting and ready to be swiped.

'I've got no place to call my own.' Sharing a bedroom can be tough as you grow older. Apart from the homework/studying issue, we all need somewhere to sit and think and chill. So talk to your parents in case a room could be freed up for you. They might be more positive about the idea if you offer to clear it out, help to redecorate and move as much of your stuff as you can. If there's no ideal solution – like a spare room you can have – make the most of your half of the bedroom by ensuring it's as cosy and tidy as possible, so it reflects your personal tastes and feels like your space. When your sibling's out, grab the opportunity to enjoy the privacy while you can.

Things to remember if they're *still* driving you crazy ...

• Their bad moods are probably nothing to do with you. Everyone has their own worries and stresses, and sometimes that can make people grouchy or act unfairly.

• It's not all grumpiness and shouting. You do have lots of fun and cosy times too, so try to remember those.

• Even annoying brothers and sisters have their good points too.

• Older siblings can be a good source of advice (have you ever tried asking?).

• Your family knows you better than anyone, and you can be completely yourself when you're with them.

• Even supposedly 'perfect' families have their rows and blow-ups too (you just don't see them!).

• Your parents are doing their best, even if they're not perfect (and whose are, anyway?).

• They love you to bits (yes, really!).

How to get great grades

Like so many things, it's all about being prepared and giving yourself the very best chance to succeed. These pointers will set you on your way ...

If you don't understand something, ask. Learning is a bit like a pyramid — the bottom layer, the basics, has to be in place first. No one will laugh at you for not knowing something, or asking for it to be explained again. Teachers are usually happy to spend extra time with you.

Start studying in plenty of time. In fact, earlier than you think you really need to. Last-minute cramming is stressful, as trying to memorize too many facts at once just fuddles the brain and makes it feel like it's going to burst.

Make a revision timetable. Figure out where you can slot in the odd chunk of studying time, and stick to it. This sort of forward planning makes life so much easier. Even if it doesn't come naturally, you can train yourself to be a super-organized girl.

Hide away. Make sure you have somewhere quiet and peaceful to study. Background music can help, but TV is distracting.

Give yourself a set time to revise – then take a break and do something nice. You deserve it, and you'll come back to your studying feeling more refreshed.

Everyone has their own studying techniques. You might prefer to re-read, then write out your notes, condensing them to the most important points. You can then reduce them even more and come up with key words that act as memory triggers. These will help you recall the rest of the info that's neatly stored away in the amazing filing cabinet that is your brain.

Test yourself – or be tested. Once you're confident that the vital info's all in your head, you might like to get together with a friend and test each other.

When you're feeling fed up ... remind yourself that you're working towards a goal. Once it's over, you can relax. You won't be huddled over your books forever.

Don't leave the bits you don't enjoy. It's tempting to avoid the really tricky or more boring stuff. But if you're finding something hard, this is the area to focus on most.

Ignore anyone who teases you or calls you a swot. They're not worth one iota of your time. In your heart of hearts, wouldn't you rather pick up that test paper feeling confident instead of quaking with nerves?

Before a big test ...

Try to have a normal evening before it, doing something relaxing.

Get a good night's sleep. No point in staying up late, revising and panicking at this stage.

Make sure you have everything you need, and your bag already packed, the night before.

Think of all the nice things you'll be able to do once it's over.

Allow yourself plenty of time to get there, and remind yourself that you're just going to do your best. That's all anyone can ask of you.

Six sassy, school-friendly hairstyles

School-day hair has to be quick and easy — but that doesn't have to mean boring. If you're in the mood for a change, why not try one of these speedy ideas?

• • • Messy bun • • • • • • • • • ♥
Works with: long hair, with or without a fringe

Brush out your hair and secure into a fairly low ponytail with a hair band. Then, as you twist the band as if you're securing your ponytail again, pull the hair just halfway through so it's caught in a bun. Tweak the bun with your fingers to make it slightly messy and, if there are too many longer strands hanging down at the back, take a hair grip and pin them up just above the bun.

• • • Half-up, half-down • • • • • • • • ♥
Works with: long hair, with or without a fringe

Take a small section of hair from one side of your face and brush through, then twist it slightly. Still holding it in one hand, take a similar-sized section from the other side and twist it, then bring them together at the back and secure with a band. Gorgeous and face-flattering.

Band and pony
Works with: long and medium-length hair

Pull your hair back and secure in a small ponytail or bun. Now put on a stretchy hair band to hold any loose strands off your face for a super-neat look.

• • •**Side plait** • • • • • • • • • ♥
Works with: long and medium-length hair

Gather your hair back and slightly to the side then start plaiting, bring the plait round and to the front over your shoulder as you go. Tie off with a hair band.

Skinny plait • • • • • • • • • ♥
Works with: medium hair, without a fringe

Comb your hair into a side parting, then take a small section from the front of your hair and plait it carefully, taking it round towards your ear. Secure your skinny plait with a clip.

• • • Side-swept sleek • • • • • • ♥

Works with: short hair, with a longish or growing-out fringe

After washing, create a sharp side parting and blow dry your hair, finishing with a little spray-on shine. If your fringe is long, add a clip to pin it back Super-cute!

• • • Messy pixie • • • • • • • • ♥

Works with: short hair

Use a hairdryer until your hair's about half-way dry, then switch off the heat and finish drying by ruffling your hair with your fingers. For a messy, textured look, work through a tiny amount of hair wax or putty, fluffing it towards your face until you have the choppy texture you want.

Your perfect school-day style ...

... is fast and fuss-free
... doesn't use too much product
... is kind to your hair (if you use straighteners now and again, spritz on some heat protector first)
... works with your hair's natural texture
... will stay looking good all day

How to smell gorgeous

While some fragrances can be eye-wateringly strong and overpowering, there are plenty of ways to smell gorgeous in a more subtle and natural way. Trouble is, how to decide what's right for you when there are so many scented goodies out there? Here's what's what in the wonderful world of scents ...

How do I know what's right for me?

Eau de Parfum is slightly stronger than Eau de Toilette, but both are pretty potent (and pricy too). A body spray (or body mist) is a lighter form of fragrance that you can spray on quite happily without worrying that it's too strong. It's more purse-friendly too.

Help – I still can't choose ...

Fragrances tend to fall into categories. They can be light and sporty, fresh and fruity, floral and girlie, or spicy and exotic. Try a few testers in a store, on those little tester cards if they have them. If you're trying them directly on your skin, two is probably enough to test in one day. Any more than that and your nose will get muddled. Lighter fragrances tend to be best on hot summer days.

Ew! Whenever I test a fragrance, it's always super-strong ...

Fragrance usually is strong when you first spray it on. Wait a few minutes until it settles, then sniff again in half an hour or so, once the powerful 'top note' has evaporated. Only then will you be able to pick up the true fragrance.

Can't I just choose what my friend uses?
It smells great on her ...
Sadly not. Perfume smells different on everyone, depending on your body's chemistry and the balance of your skin.

And when I've found my perfect fragrance?
Don't put on too much. A tiny amount is enough to give you a lovely, fresh scent. If you wear it often, it'll become your own signature scent – unique to you.

Other ways to smell gorgeous
Body lotions often smell lovely and give a faint fragrance for an hour or two after you've applied them.

Solid perfume usually comes in a little pot. It's handy for travelling, especially if you're flying and can't take liquids in the cabin. A tiny dab on your wrists is usually enough.

Perfumed oils are also lovely dabbed onto the wrists where the warmth of your skin brings out the fragrance.

Three tips to steal

Although it's great to have your favourite fragrance, do follow your instincts and spray on whatever you feel like, according to what feels right. 'I wear a million different fragrances,' says singer Taylor Swift, 'so it just depends on what I randomly pick.'

Different plant scents can have a powerful effect on how you feel (for instance, vanilla and lavender are soothing, while citrus scents have an enlivening effect). If you find one you love, it may be because it triggers happy memories: when she was creating her first fragrance, actress Jennifer Aniston wanted to include the scent of jasmine which she remembered smelling at night when she was growing up in California.

Hollywood icon Marilyn Monroe loved Chanel No. 5 so much, she wore the classic fragrance to bed. A quick spritz of body spray on your pillow will give you equally sweet-smelling dreams.

How to make a gorgeous face mask

Face masks are a real treat that can help soften and nourish your skin. Of course, you can buy ready-made face masks — the ones that come in sachets are fun for a sleepover. But making your own costs pennies, and you know they're 100% natural. Sure, they're messy and gloopy, but that's half the fun.

Before you apply your mask, wash your face and tie back your hair, so it doesn't get caked in gunk. Avoiding the delicate eye area, leave your mask on for 10-15 minutes, then wash off thoroughly with warm water and pat your skin dry.

Here are five scrumptious recipes to try:

Green gloop

Avocados are rich in nourishing oils, so great for softening normal and dry skins. It looks, well … a little bogeyish, to be frank, but don't let that put you off.

What you need

- Half a ripe, squishy avocado
- 3 teaspoons runny honey.

Mash the avocado with a fork until it's fairly smooth, then add the honey. It'll be a lovely gloopy consistency that's easy to smear on.

Banana blend

Bananas nourish and soften, and they mash down easily to a pulpy sludge. The lemon juice makes this ideal for oily to normal skin types.

What you need

- One small ripe banana
- A tablespoon of honey
- A few drops of lemon juice.

Mash your banana until it's just squidgy (too runny and it will be hard to smear on). Add your honey and lemon juice and slap it on.

Oaty mush

This is a great cleansing mask for all skin types, plus the oaty bits give it a grainy texture. Massage it in gently using small circular movements, for a light exfoliating effect, which brightens the skin.

What you need

- A couple of handfuls of fine oatmeal (from supermarkets or health food shops)
- Two tablespoons natural live yogurt
- A teaspoon of runny honey.

Mix the ingredients, adding the yogurt bit by bit until your mixture is soft and easily spreadable.

How to give a great speech

Speaking in public is scary but, with a little preparation, no one will guess you're nervous. You'll come across as calm, well-informed and confident — an expert speaker, in fact!

Before your speech ...

Prepare. While it's far better to do a speech without reading from a sheet of paper, it's a good idea to make notes. You can go through these to make sure you've covered all the points you want to make. You might also realize that some aren't needed, or are repetitive, so you can cut these out. Remember: the most powerful speeches have a direct, simple message. They shouldn't be too complicated.

Write down some brain-jogging key words on a card. These will act as reminders of your main points. You can keep your card somewhere in view, should you need it, or you can actually hold it. This acts as a kind of security blanket — or like one of those people in the wings at a theatre, ready to whisper a line if an actor forgets one. In fact, chances are you'll hardly need to glance at your card at all.

Rehearse. Try out your speech on someone who'll give constructive criticism and ask them: was I too fast or too slow? Is the speech too long or too short? Is there anything I need to make clearer, or anything I should cut out?

During your speech ...

Relax your body. Try not to stand rigidly as it'll make you look like you're quaking with nerves. Relax your shoulders and don't be afraid to use your hands to emphasize points you're making.

Use your eyes. This doesn't mean staring hard at one person in the audience until they're squirming in their seat. It's better to glance around the audience. That way, people feel involved and connected to you.

Slow down! When you're nervous, your breath tends to come shallow and fast, making you sound breathless. Try to keep your breathing steady, and talk a tiny bit slower than you would normally.

Think positive thoughts. Keep telling yourself: I can do this as well as anyone else. Also, it helps to remind yourself that it's only five, ten (or however many) minutes and of course a clued-up, capable girl like you can handle that. Imagine people telling you how well you've done afterwards.

Smile. Not constantly — that might look a bit weird — but now and again, so you come across as friendly, engaging and someone people want to listen to.

Keep looking at your audience. Staring down at the floor gives the impression that you just want it to be over ...

Keep it in proportion. It's only a speech, after all. While you want to do as well as you possibly can, the odd stutter or stumble over a word really doesn't matter. People aren't sitting there, waiting for you to make a mistake — they're on your side, and want to see you do your very best. Remember that you're incredibly courageous for getting up there at all.

How to zap a blemish

Argh – a spot always seems to pop up when you least want it. But don't panic – it's not going to be there forever. Here's the low-down on zits, and how to persuade that blemish to fade away super-quick.

My skin used to be clear, so where are all these spots coming from?

Annoyingly, spots are just a part of growing up. There are major hormonal changes as you go through puberty, including the production of an oily substance called sebum. Everyone's skin makes sebum – it keeps your complexion soft and supple. But when there's too much of it, your pores can become blocked, which leads to blackheads and spots. While a healthy diet helps to keep your skin healthy, the odd bag of chips doesn't cause spots. It's just your developing body, doing its thing.

That doesn't make me feel any better ...

Of course not – but do remember it's a phase that most people grow out of.

So what can I do right now?

Let's start with some don'ts. Please don't prod or pick at spots – it doesn't help them to heal any faster (in fact it only makes them look redder and angrier). Squeezing can cause tiny scars, and even if you manage to get rid of a spot, another one often pops up in the same place. So what to do? Make sure you keep your skin clean with a gentle facial wash to lessen the chances of pores becoming clogged. Avoid harsh, oil-stripping cleansers as these can encourage your skin to produce even more oil. For the actual zit, apply a dab of anti-bacterial spot lotion or gel every morning and night. This will encourage the spot to dry out quickly, and speed up the healing process. Gently exfoliating once or twice a week (with a product formulated for young, spot-prone skins) can help too.

Can I cover up my spot?

Yes, with a little medicated concealer — the kind that also helps to heal spots. It's best to gently pat it on, rather than rubbing it in. But remember that spots heal more quickly when exposed to the air, so don't cake them with make-up.

What about blackheads?

These tiny dark dots are just pores blocked with sebum. You can squeeze these, if you're extra-careful: fill the washbasin with hot (not boiling) water and hold your face over it for a few moments (this helps to open the pores, making blackheads easier to remove). Then, using the pads of your (clean) fingers and never your nails, gently squeeze the area around the blackhead.

If it doesn't pop out easily, leave it alone as frantic squeezing leaves nasty nail marks, and can even damage your skin. When you've finished, splash your face with cold water to close the pores, and gently pat dry with a towel.

I still wish my skin was clear, like it used to be ...
Remind yourself that a spot is never as noticeable to other people as it is to you. So emphasize your gorgeous features, like your eyes or smile, and never let a pesky zit dent your confidence.

How to make a friend feel gorgeous

So your best friend's down in the dumps? It won't take much to put a smile back on her face. Here are 20 easy ways to show you care …

1. Send a text telling her how great she is.

2. If she wants to grumble, cry or have a good moan, then let her. Listen, and resist the urge to keep butting in. You don't even need to offer advice – just being there is enough.

3. Coax her out of the house. Just going for a walk, chatting in the park or stopping off for a drink and a cake will lift her spirits.

4. Make her laugh. Share something embarrassing or stupid that's happened to you, or remind her of something hilarious that had you both in hysterics.

5. Bake her some cookies, perhaps with a special message piped on. Presents always mean so much more when they're hand-made and personal.

6. Don't assume it's you who's making her sad. If you genuinely think you're in the wrong, though, give her a big hug and say sorry.

7. Be patient if she says she needs time alone. Again, that's no reflection on you.

8. Make her a friendship bracelet and wrap it prettily.

9. Everyone has a certain feature that makes them beautiful and unique. Don't be afraid to complement a friend and tell her how pretty she is.

10. Give her your full attention – don't break off a conversation to read a text or answer a call.

11. Suggest doing something different like ice skating, a dance class or joining a drama club together. Learning a new skill, or discovering a talent, is great for boosting confidence, and it might help her to forget her worries too.

12. If your friend asks for advice, try to make suggestions without sounding too bossy. So, rather than saying, 'You should do this,' you could say something like, 'It might be a good idea to …' or, 'Perhaps you could try …' Reassure her that you truly believe she'll make the right decision.

13. Make sure you return anything she lends you promptly and in good condition.

14. Watch a sweet, girlie movie together. There's nothing like getting lost in a story to chase those blues away. A bowl of fresh, warm popcorn is a must ...

15. Give your friend a relaxing head massage. Using the pads of your fingers and thumbs, work in slow, gentle circles over the scalp. Keep the pressure firm, but don't press too hard. It might take a bit of getting used to, but once you've mastered it, it's one of the most soothing things you can do.

16. Offer to give her a manicure or pedicure. Sure, she can do these for herself — but having someone else do it feels so treaty.

17. Bring her out on a dog walk, borrowing a pet if you need to, as being close to animals has been proven to have a mood-lifting effect. It's hard to be sad when you're throwing a ball for a dog …

18. Pick her a bunch of flowers from your garden.

19. Don't brush off her problems or dismiss them as trivial. The trick is to acknowledge that her worries are real to her, while helping her to keep them in proportion (tricky!).

20. Remind her that you're always there for her, no matter what.

How to display your gorgeous photos

It's all very well having your pics on your phone, but sometimes you want to make a special display of your favourites. And what better way to cheer up your room than with the shots that make you smile? Try these ...

Doodly frames

You can pick up a whiteboard and wipe-off pens really cheaply, then change your display whenever the mood takes you. Just stick your pictures on your board with Blu-tack, then draw wiggly frames around them with your pens. Drawing really ornate frames — the kind your see framing those stern, old-fashioned portraits in stately homes — is really effective when your photos are all smiley and modern. Doodle to your heart's content — maybe ask a friend to help and make it a joint project.

It's you, clearly

Clear plastic photo holders — the kind with lots of pockets for pics — look great hung up on a bedroom door. Instead of filling every compartment with a photo, you can vary things by slipping other treasures into some of the pockets.

Pin-board mash-up

If you have a pin board or cork board, pin up your favourite photos, surrounded by lots of other little things you like — such as tickets, hand-written notes, favourite birthday cards, tiny mirrors and pictures cut out of magazines. It looks especially good if some of your bits and pieces are three dimensional – try tiny soft toys, bits of jewellery or fake flowers. The idea is to cram on as much as you can – the more the merrier. The quirky, colourful drawing pins you find in stationery stores will make it look even better.

Collage girls

You'll need a large clip frame (or any old photo frame) for this. Take out the backing card and carefully position your photos to make a collage. Some will look good with the people cut out, and it's fun to play with scale – try a big close-up of a face next to a teeny full-length picture. Move them around until you're happy, then stick them down with dabs of glue stick and put back in the frame.

Peg 'em up

If you have some tiny coloured pegs – like the kind used on washing lines, but mini – you can secure a length of string or wool along a shelf or window frame and peg up your favourite pics.

Other cute things to display in frames

You can pick up old frames in charity shops and take out the picture. Then cut your own background to size, using card, fabric or felt, and make your own art by displaying ...

... beachy finds, such as tiny shells, pebbles and starfish secured with strong glue * those delicate leaf skeletons you sometimes find in autumn * pressed flowers * your own drawings and doodles * all the bits and pieces you collected from a special holiday.

How to choose the perfect hairstyle - - - - - -

The best hairstyle for you is one that works easily with your natural hair type and texture (that is: fine or thick, straight, wavy or curly, or somewhere in between). Otherwise it'll require heaps of effort from you, and will never quite look the way you'd imagined it. Don't be afraid to chat to your hairdresser until you've agreed on the perfect cut – that way, it'll stay looking great with minimum fuss.

Before the cut ...

Choose your hairdresser with care (generally, recommendations from friends are your best guide). A hair salon should be friendly and welcoming – not scary or intimidating.

Have a fair idea of what you'd like. Magazines are full of ideas, or you might be inspired by a friend's style. The clearer you are, the easier it'll be to communicate to your hairdresser.

Think about your lifestyle and how much time you want to spend on your hair. Your ideal style should look great without any fiddling about (you can always do the works – straightening, curling, pinning it up – for special occasions). If you're a sporty girl, it makes sense to opt for a short cut, or one that's long enough to tie back, as in-between lengths can be annoying when they flap in your face.

Using your face shape as a guide

To work out which face shape you are, scrape back your hair — including your fringe — and study your reflection front-on.

An **oval** face looks great with pretty much any style. Long, medium or a cute crop — all lengths suit you as you're not trying to balance out any particular feature.

For a **heart-shaped** face (a broad forehead narrowing down to a dainty chin), it's best to avoid styles that make your forehead look wider.

A **square** face has a strong jaw — softer, wispier and longer styles will help to soften the angles.

For a **round** face, it's a good idea to avoid chin-length bobs which can emphasize the roundness. Consider choosing a longer style instead.

When you go for your cut ...

Show your hairdresser a picture of the style you like, if you have one. A stylist should take the time to chat with you, and examine your hair while it's dry. She shouldn't rush you off to the basins.

Watch exactly what your hairdresser is doing as she dries and finishes your hair. Treat it like a styling lesson. Asking questions at this stage can help you to achieve the same look at home. Don't feel pressurized to buy salon-priced products, though. You can figure out what you need once you've washed it yourself and got used to your new style.

If you don't like it? Panic not – freshly cut and styled hair sometimes

feels a bit odd, just because it's different. Give yourself time to get used to it and, if you still don't like it, try a different salon next time. Meanwhile, experiment with clips and hair accessories, finding a nice way of wearing it until it's time for your next cut.

A note about fringes

Fringes can be really flattering, making your eyes look amazing and drawing attention away from a broad forehead. A wispy, choppy or side-swept one tends to be the most flattering, although a sharp, straight-across fringe can look dramatic, if that's the effect you want. Remember that a fringe will need regular trims, and take a few months to grow out if you don't like it (you can always clip it to the side in the meantime). Most good hairdressers will give free fringe trims between cuts.

A note about colour

A permanent tint's a scary proposition. Your natural shade is the one that truly suits your colouring, and if you don't like a tint, it's difficult to have it re-dyed to bring you back to your own hair colour. Plus, as it grows out, there's the issue of contrasting roots. If you want to experiment with colour, go for a temporary one that gradually fades over several washes.

How to have a gorgeous sleepover

Hours of chat, laughs and gossiping with your best friends ... is anything better than that? Here are some ideas to make it extra-special.

Before the big night ...

Your friends: It's best to invite a smallish group (say, four at the most) for that cosy, secret-sharing feel. Choose friends who all know each other well — a sleepover's not really the time to introduce someone new, who might feel like a bit of an outsider. Remind everyone to bring a sleeping bag and pillow — plus their PJs and a toothbrush of course.

Your room: A good clear-out and tidy will ensure there's plenty of floor space for the cushions, futon, bedroll or whatever your friends are going to sleep on. It'll also make it a more relaxing place to hang out in — and you'll be able to find all the things you'll need (nail polishes, make-up, favourite DVDs and so on).

Your plans: Have a think about what you'd like to eat and do. While it's probably enough just to be together, it'll be even better if you've put some thought into it. Stock up on sweets for your midnight feast — it's a good idea to buy a big bag of fortune cookies too (from a Chinese supermarket), so you can giggle over the messages inside.

Ten things to do on the night

Customize **pizzas.** Buy plain pizza bases, and make sure you have tomato purée plus toppings like grated cheese, sliced mushrooms, ham, salami and olives, so everyone can create their own.

Make a **movie.** Write a script and make costumes or keep it simple and tell the story of your friendship.

Face masks (see p. 100-101) and **facials** (see p. 146-147) are perfect for sleepovers, when you have time to pamper and indulge.

A **chocolate fondue** is lip-smackingly delicious. In a heavy-based pan, slowly heat 130 ml milk, 120 ml double cream and 200 g dark chocolate broken up into bits (the posh, 70% cocoa kind). Stir until it's all blended, then transfer into a large bowl. Have strawberries, mini marshmallows, banana slices and tiny cubes of chocolate brownie, set out on a plate with skewers for non-messy dunking.

Manicures and **pedicures** are a lovely way to feel pampered. Ask your friends to bring their nail polishes/pens so you can all get creative.

Hair braiding. Plaits are cute, which is probably why girls have experimented with them since medieval times. Either plait the whole head or, for speed, just a small section close to the face.

Tell **ghost stories.** Dig out your scariest books, turn the lights down low and all huddle up together for a fright-fest. If you don't have any spooky books, get everyone to take turns in telling spine-chilling true stories.

Smoothies are delicious and, if you're organized, everyone can pick their favourite ingredients and create their own. Most smoothies either have a juice base (like apple or pineapple juice), or a dairy base (milk, plain yogurt or ice cream). Then just throw in your favourite fruit and whizz it up in the blender. Stuck for ideas? Try 1 cup plain yogurt blended with 1 ripe banana, 2 cups strawberries and 1 cup raspberries. Using frozen fruit makes your smoothie nice and chilled (or you can add ice cubes to the mix), and a little honey adds sweetness if you need it.

Movie time. Having a theme (like scary, funny or rom-coms) can be useful if you can't decide what to watch.

Share secrets. (Remembering to keep them, of course ...)

Making sure everyone gets along ...
Chances are, everyone'll have a fantastic night. But just to make sure ...

Remember that, while everyone might say they want to watch a scary movie, some of your friends could be a bit freaked, but too embarrassed to say so.

Don't force anyone to share a secret if it's obvious they don't really want to.

Be kind and sensitive, especially if a friend isn't used to being away from home over overnight.

How to look gorgeous in photos

A red-carpet stance looks far too posey. Your true gorgeousness will shine out if you're relaxed and natural. Here's how:

• Rather than worrying about having a 'perfect' smile, just think about something that makes you laugh or feel warm and happy inside. That way, your smile will be unforced and natural, which is always the loveliest kind.

• 'Red-eye' happens when the flash illuminates your retina (the lining of your eye). Although most cameras have an anti-red-eye setting, you can lessen the chances of it happening by looking slightly above the lens rather than straight at it.

• Natural daylight is more flattering than flash, which can be harsh. Likewise, overcast days (or weak sun) are more photo-friendly than dazzling sun. On a bright day, try not to face the sun or you'll squint.

• Sheer, neutral shades look better than tons of make-up in pics.

• Try to relax your body, while still having good posture (this means not slumping or slouching).

• Tell yourself you look great and allow your natural beauty to be captured forever. *Cheese!*

How to look gorgeous in vintage

Quirky, eye-catching and utterly unique – what's not to love about vintage? Charity shops can be treasure troves, and you can even pick up the odd outfit at jumble and car boot sales. Keep your eyes peeled for vintage clothing fairs visiting your town too – and if an older relative is having a clear-out, ask if you can have first pick and nab yourself a star find …

Allow yourself plenty of time – and have patience. Some days you'll find loads of great stuff. Other days, it'll all be sad, bobbly knitwear and droopy old skirts. Squirrelling out something special is half the fun, so check those rails carefully to make sure you don't miss anything.

Some charity shops arrange clothes in colours, so it's easier to hone in, missile-like, on your favourite shades. But don't dismiss those chaotic shops where everything's all muddled up. This is often where bargains lie.

Even if something's a little wild and crazy, it might be worth snapping up just for fun. Kylie's famous gold hotpants were a charity-shop find, and actress Sienna Miller has been spotted in amazing vintage gowns.

Charity shops in posh areas tend to have brilliant stuff, so it's worth checking out different neighbourhoods. In parts of towns where lots of students live, there tends to be a lot of competition for the best bits.

You can usually try things on in charity shops. It's worth the effort, as you're unlikely to be able to return it if you change your mind.

Don't expect to find what everyone else is wearing, as the joy of vintage is that it's original and one-off. As Lily Allen puts it, it's all about: 'trying to re-create different looks which aren't just about merging with every other girl on the high street.' Plus, vintage clothes are often far better quality too. They've lasted for decades, after all.

Not sure what to look for? Be inspired by fashion magazines and blogs and, when you've bought something a bit adventurous, try it on with clothes you already own. Mixing it up with high street buys is a gentle way to ease vintage into your wardrobe.

Don't just hunt for clothes. You can find brilliant bags, scarves, hats and jewellery to give you a dash of vintage style even if you don't feel like going for the whole, full-on look.

How to expand your friendship circle

Maybe you and your best friend aren't as close as you were. Or perhaps you feel like shaking things up and getting to know some new people (after all, you can never have too many friends). So how to go about it?

Be friendly and approachable. If you're feeling shy, it's easy to come across as slightly aloof. But if you can relax, smile and just say 'hi', you're well on the way to getting to know someone new.

Remember that they might be shy too. Just because someone hasn't spoken to you doesn't mean they wouldn't like to be friends.

Be open-minded. Even if someone is into different things, they can still become a buddy. Wouldn't it be a boring world if all your friends were alike?

Look out for the new girl. Starting a new school can be hard, so why not make it easier by offering to show her around, or asking if she'd like to sit with you at lunch?

Try something new. It's the best way to boost your social life and get to know a whole different group. Plus, you'll learn a new skill or build on a talent too.

Be sensitive to your old friends' feelings … but don't let them dictate who you spend time with. Sometimes, old friends act a little weird and possessive when you make new mates. They might feel threatened, or worry that you prefer this new girl to them. While you should reassure your old friends that you'll always be there for them, don't let anyone make you feel bad for branching out. As long as you still see your old friends one-to-one sometimes – and don't make them feel shunned or left out – then you haven't done anything wrong.

Ask questions. When you're getting to know someone new, it's important to show you're interested in their life (without firing so many questions that it feels like a scary interview, of course). It's also a good way to discover what you have in common.

When you've picked the wrong person … *Eek!* Sometimes, you might befriend someone, only to discover that they're not your kind of person after all. It's tricky to step away when you've been all friendly, so tread carefully. Still include them, but in a group rather than one-to-one. Encourage them to mix with as many people as possible so, hopefully, they'll soon find a best friend of their own.

Friendship blips

What to do when a new friend — or any friend — turns tricky …

 She keeps asking to borrow your stuff. There's nothing wrong with telling a little white lie and saying you need it, and can't lend it at the moment. Or just say a simple: 'Sorry, I'd rather not lend that out.' Then quickly move on to talk about something else.

She always expects you to do what she wants to do. Again, be polite but firm: 'Sorry, I don't really feel like doing that right now.' A little give and take is essential to any friendship, but you should never feel as if you're just tagging along like an obedient puppy.

She badmouths another friend. Explain that you really like that person, and don't want to get into saying negative things about her.

She wants to copy your work. Remind her that it's not going to help her, and that it's usually obvious when someone's copied. Plus, what if you've made mistakes and she copies them too? Try to boost her confidence and help her to realize she can manage her own work perfectly well without copying.

She copies your style. This can be very flattering. Annoying, too. Why not have a make-over session where you help her to discover her own individual look?

How to make colour work for you

Colour can have an amazing effect, not just on how you look, but how you feel too. The best way to discover which colours suit you is to hold them up against your face, in natural daylight. While certain shades might drain you, making you look tired and peaky, others will put a healthy glow into your cheeks. If you're not brave enough for an eye-popping shade, then wear just a flash of it, teamed with neutral basics.

What's your shade?

Pink is calming, good for confidence and is thought to make us feel more secure. A splash of pink can be flattering to your face, and pale pastel shades look yummy against darker skins.

Green is another soothing colour. Vivid emerald is a favourite shade for red-heads, but murky greens can be tricky against your face.

Orange symbolizes freedom and looks amazing against darker skins. It's a feel-good colour that can't help but rev up your mood.

Blue is calming, positive and is believed to make people more creative. From pale sky blue to deepest indigo, it's an easy colour to wear and suits everyone.

Red looks great against pale and dark skins alike, and has a brilliant, mood-lifting effect. It also shouts, 'Look at me!'

Yellow can be another tricky one, as it can drain the face of colour. It's gorgeous against darker skins, though, and adds a pop of sunny colour that can really lift a look. A more muted mustard shade can give you a cool, retro edge.

Purple is a bold, confident colour that says you're free-spirited and creative. Incredibly easy to wear, it suits all skin tones and looks striking with black.

Black can be chic, elegant, dramatic or mysterious, and works well with any colour. Mixing it up with another shade is usually more flattering (and interesting) than wearing top-to-toe black.

Grey is a restful colour. You might think it's drab but it's surprisingly warming against the skin, making you look healthy and glowing. For wardrobe basics, dark charcoal grey makes a nice alternative to black.

Brown might sound icky, but warm, chocolate shades can be especially flattering and, like dark grey, are a handy alternative black.

White symbolizes peace and serenity – as long as you don't splatter bolognaise sauce down the front. It's a calming colour that looks great with all skin tones, and if you're on holiday it really enhances your tan. So don't forget to pack those snowy-white T-shirts …

How to be gorgeous on holiday

All your summery beauty questions answered ... so you come back more gorgeous than ever!

Do I really need sunscreen?

Sorry, but yes, as sunburn is no joke at all. Luckily, not all sunscreens are gloopy and greasy – there are plenty of light sprays that do the job just as well. So squirt on ...

Do I have to?

Yes again – and here's why. There are two types of sun rays – UVA, which cause long-term damage such as wrinkles, and UVB, the baddies that cause sunburn. Your sunscreen should protect against both with a high SPF (sun protection factor): go for at least SPF 30 if you're fair, and SPF 20 if you're darker skinned. Apply at least 15 minutes before you go out in the sun, and again after you've been swimming. Don't forget those little areas where the sun can sneak up on you – like your ears, and around the legs of your swimsuit in case it shifts a bit, exposing vulnerable skin. A sunhat will protect your scalp: yes, it can still burn, even though it's covered by hair. Sunburn on your parting can be especially tender and painful.

What about my face?

Best to use a very high SPF. Who wants a glowing beacon nose? You probably don't need to use moisturizer day to day, but on holiday,

with the sun and sea water, you might notice dry, flaky patches springing up. Just use a little light, lotion-type moisturizer on any dry bits after washing your face in the morning and at night. The sun and sea can dry out lips too, so pop a nourishing lip balm in your beach bag.

What if it's not that sunny?

Sun rays are very determined and can even get through hazy cloud, so always use your sunscreen.

And what if it's scorching?

Avoid being out in the sun between midday and 2 pm, when the rays are strongest, and stay hydrated too. Fizzy drinks are tempting but water is best – it'll help to keep your energy levels up too.

What should I do if I burn?

Ouch. Use plenty of cooling aftersun lotion, and cover up until it's all healed. Loose cotton fabrics are softer and kinder against sun-frazzled skin.

My hair gets dry and frizzy on holiday. What can I do about that?

Salt water and pool water can make it dry and hungry for conditioner, so remember to pack some in your case. It'll thank you for a deep conditioning treatment too, around halfway through your holiday.

Is it important to wear sunglasses?

Yes, for protection against sun damage – and also because bright sunlight causes you to squint. Oh, and sunnies look pretty cool too.

How to give fruit a touch of gorgeousness

Okay, fruit is pretty gorgeous. It's fresh, natural and packed with vitamins ... but sometimes it feels as if it's just there, sitting in its bowl and looking at you. And occasionally it's nice to shake things up a bit, making sure you still get your five-a-day, but in slightly more interesting way.

Choc-dipped strawberries

1. Wash and dry some plump, juicy strawberries, then pour about 3 cm of water in a saucepan and bring it to a gentle boil. Turn off the heat.

2. Put around 150 g milk chocolate drops (or buttons) into a heat-proof bowl and carefully place the bowl in the pan, making sure no water comes up the sides and into your bowl.

3. When your choc has melted, give it a stir. Then dip strawberries in, so they're half-covered in chocolate.

4. Place them on a tray covered in greaseproof paper or baking parchment to dry, or pop them in the fridge if you want them to firm up faster.

Fruity frozen yogurt

Here's a super-healthy alternative to ice cream. It looks beautiful and has none of those artificial colours, sweeteners or preservatives that can make you feel a little bit crazy. This is also a great way to use up slightly mushy fruit.

1. Take 150 g of your favourite frozen berries (a mixture of strawberries, raspberries and blueberries is yum) and 250 g of plain yogurt straight from the fridge.

2. Fling them into a blender with a tablespoon of runny honey, and give it a good blitz – it'll take quite a while to become smooth.

3. Taste to see if it's sweet enough and if not, give it another whizz with more honey.

4. Eat at once (there'll be enough for you and a couple of friends) or store in a tub in the freezer. If you prefer, keep it in the fridge: it'll go slightly runny but makes a lovely pink sauce for ice cream.

Fruity kebabs

Cut your favourite fruits — like melon, mango, orange, pineapple and kiwi — into chunks and thread on to wooden skewers in dazzling colour combinations.

Other fruity ideas ...

• Decorate mocktails with cherries, strawberries or slices of orange threaded on to cocktails sticks.

• Cherries taste amazing in cola — try it!

• Freeze freshly-squeezed juice (or juice from a carton) to make the yummiest ice lollies.

• Pop a mini fruit salad in your lunchbox.

• Split some bananas, place a sliver of chocolate in each and wrap in foil. Bake on a low heat for ten minutes or so, or until the chocolate's melted.

Fruity freeze

Make your ice cubes prettier by dropping a berry (raspberry, blueberry, sliver of strawberry, whatever) into each of your ice cube tray compartments, then fill with water and freeze. Use to perk up your drinks.

How to make a little make-up seem like lots

Looking lovely is more to do with the way you apply make-up than having a huge choice of goodies at your fingertips. What's more, the most versatile, hard-working products can double up and do at least two different jobs – clever, huh? What you do need, though, are brushes, as applying make-up with your fingers transfers oil onto your face, which can cause make-up to crease and smear. Get hold of a fine eye-liner brush, a slightly larger one for eye shadow (or a pack of sponge-tipped applicators), a round blusher blush and a slightly larger powder brush and you're ready to go.

Some clever multi-taskers

• Eye shadow as eyeliner ... Dampen a dark shade of pressed powder eye shadow with a moist eyeliner brush, then paint a fine line as close as possible to your upper lashes. You can try this with dry eye shadow too. Deep, smoky greys, browns, purples and navy shades work well, especially when toned with your base eye shadow (try a light mauve to cover over your lids, then a line of dark plum liner). It's also a handy way of using those dark shades, which are too dramatic to be worn all over your eyelid.

• Lip colour as blush ... Using your fingers, stroke a little sheer, creamy lip colour onto the 'apples' (the pump parts) of your cheeks for a peachy glow.

• Clear mascara as brow definer ... Wipe off nearly all the mascara with a tissue, then sweep the brush over each brow in the direction of its growth (from nose to ear). Voilà — tamed, tidy brows.

• Eyeliner as brow pencil ... Use light, feather strokes of brown pencil (light, mid- or dark brown, depending on your colouring), following the direction of the hair growth. You can use brown eye shadow to define brows too — just brush on a little to give definition.

• Eyeliner as eye shadow ... Using a very soft pencil, shade the area close to your upper lashes, then smudge carefully with a sponge-tipped applicator.

• Eye shadow or blusher as bronzer ... Using a shimmery shade and a large blusher or powder brush, sweep a little onto your shoulders or cheekbones — lovely with a tan.

• New shades for lips ... If you have a couple of lippies you're not too keen on, try blending them together with a brush to make a prettier colour.

• And of course, tinted moisturizer is a classic multi-tasker, as it gives a little coverage as well as keeping your skin baby-soft.

How to shake off your worries

Worries are weird things. They start off small, then grow bigger and bigger until there's no space in your head to think about anything else. Try these ten ways to shrink that fear right back down to size until it's just a teeny dot (and no longer planet-sized).

Talk. A problem shared really is a problem halved. Pick someone you trust and tell them, if you possibly can. No one should shoulder a serious worry all on their own.

Write. Your worry, that is — in a diary, notebook or anywhere you can keep it private. You can even scribble it on a sheet of paper, then rip it up afterwards if you want to. It's the act of writing it down that's important, as this can help to make sense of it in your head.

Run. If you're feeling stressed, running really helps. It makes your body produce endorphins (also known as 'happy hormones') and gives your circulation a boost. Plus, you can think while you run, figuring out how to solve a problem – or, better still, you can switch off your racing thoughts and just 'be'. An instant head-clearer.

Sleep. In other words, don't lie there turning a worry over and over in your head, because things always seems worse late at night. Instead, take a deep breath and try to guide your thoughts towards positive things – events to look forward to, or things you've done recently that have made you feel happy and proud. Your worry will have shrunk back down by morning – guaranteed.

Reflect. Ever thought of keeping a happiness journal? It's a place to write down the things that have made you happy during the day, and it's a way of taking the time to really appreciate them. They can be tiny things, like having a laugh with a friend or finding something precious which you thought you'd lost. As you think about the good stuff, those worries start to feel less significant.

Listen. To a friend, that is, especially if something's getting her down. It can remind you that everyone has worries, and takes your mind off your own problems for a while. Also, you're helping just by listening, which will make you feel good about yourself, because you're being a true friend.

Plan. Rather than fretting and getting nowhere, try to switch on the practical part of your brain and figure out: how am I going to solve this? What's the first step I should take? It'll make you feel more empowered if you can see your way out of a problem. Try writing down your various options, with pros and cons for each, then sleep on it. You don't have to rush into making a decision.

 Laugh. Sometimes life can feel too intense. Watching a goofball comedy with friends can really perk up your mood.

Pamper. Be good to yourself because worries always seem ten times bigger when you're tired, hungry or feeling run down.

Copy. Be inspired by someone who seems to handle life's hiccups really well, and try doing what they do. For instance, you probably know someone who brushes off teasing more easily than most people can. Figure out: how does she do it? What can I learn from her? Could I do that too? This doesn't mean mimicking another person exactly. It means being inspired by someone you admire, and developing some of those qualities within yourself.

How to blow-dry your hair

While you probably don't have the time to blow-dry every day, it makes all the difference when you do. You can go for a cute, textured look, or loads of volume and bounce — the choice is yours. Once you've got the hang of it, you can set up a blow-dry bar in your bedroom next time you have a sleepover, so all your friends will look like shampoo-ad girls.

Here's how to blow dry medium-to-long hair when you want red-carpet body and bounce ...

1. After washing, towel dry your hair to blot away most of the moisture and comb through to tease out tangles.

2. Add a little volumizing product such as mousse or thickening lotion – not too much, or it'll weigh your hair down (for longish hair, a golf ball-sized blob is probably enough – less for shorter hair, obviously). Work it through with your fingers so it's evenly distributed.

3. Now start drying. With your head upside down so your hair falls to the floor, start brushing through with a large, round brush to create a little lift at the roots. Direct the dryer on to the parts you're brushing, keeping it moving and not so close to your hair that you'll scorch it.

4. When your hair's almost dry, flip your head the right way up and style your hair as normal. All it probably needs now is a final brush to make it glossy and sleek. A flat, natural-bristled brush is best for this part.

5. If you like, you can work a tiny amount of shine serum through the ends of your hair for extra gloss.

Can blow-drying damage my hair?

Not if you use a good conditioner when you wash, and keep the dryer moving. Having said that, it's best to let your hair dry naturally some days, just to give it a break.

What about blow-drying short hair?

One of the brilliant things about shorter hair is that you don't have to blow dry it. You can just towel dry, ruffle it with your fingers and perhaps work in a dab of product to give it texture. If you want to blow dry for a more chic finish, use your fingers to coax it into shape as you go.

Can I use my straighteners after blow-drying?

Yes — they're meant to be used on dry, not wet or damp hair. Try not to straighten your hair every day, though, and keep it healthy by using a protective lotion or spray each time. You don't have to straighten all of your hair either — just treating the end sections gives a lovely sleek finish.

How to treat a friend to a gorgeous facial

People pay a fortune for professional facials — but you don't have to. They're really easy to do, and although you can treat yourself to one, they're also a lovely way to pamper a friend when you're hanging out together.

What can a facial do?

... Deep-cleanse the skin so it's fresh and glowing.

... Moisturize and soften.

... Feel gorgeously relaxing and pampering.

What you need

- A hair band or scarf to tie back hair
- Cream-type cleanser
- Face mask (choose an exfoliating kind for brighter, softer skin)
- Light moisturizer
- Cotton wool balls or pads.

Four steps to glow

Cleanse ... Wash your hands and tie your friend's hair back from her face. Taking a blob of cleanser, massage it gently all over her face (apart from the delicate eye area) using the pads of your fingers. Wipe away with cotton wool.

Mask ... Now apply the face mask, spreading it thinly and evenly over your friend's face, again missing out the eye area. If it's an exfoliating face mask, massage it very gently, using small circular movements (it should never feel scratchy or rough). Pay extra attention to the nose, forehead and chin, known as the 'T-zone', which tends to be oily. Leave on for ten to 15 minutes. You can wipe away most of the mask with cotton wool, but it's probably easier for your friend to wash it off with warm water.

Tone ... Follow with a splash of cold water to tighten the pores and give a refreshing, zingy feeling.

Moisturize ... Now gently massage in a little light moisturizer to make her skin ultra-soft.

How to save time in the mornings

Ways to get out the door fast — without resorting to going to bed in your school uniform ...

• Do as much as you can the night before. That means packing your schoolbag (with homework done) and making sure your clothes are all ready and pressed.

• Keep your shoes in the same place (clean and not mud-caked) to save a frantic search when you're just about to rush out the door.

• If your hair needs a wash, but you don't have time, spray on a little dry shampoo. Leave it for a couple of minutes to absorb your hair's oils, then brush out thoroughly.

• A low ponytail always looks cute for school, perhaps with a few loose strands framing your face.

• A speedy breakfast like yogurt, banana and a slice of toast provides protein, calcium and vital carbs to keep you going 'til lunch.

• A quick slick of lip balm or gloss will make you feel more 'done'.

• Avoid turning on the TV if you can. It'll slow you down and before you know it, you'll be caught up watching it and already late ...

What to eat for gorgeous skin, hair and nails

Eating healthily nourishes your body, making it function as well as it possibly can. If you follow these tips, you'll soon notice a difference in the condition of your skin, hair and nails – plus, you'll be bursting with energy too.

So what's on the menu?

Try to include at least some of the goodies on this shopping list …

• Oily fish (like salmon, sardines and mackerel) are packed with omega-3 amino acids, which help to keep skin plumped up, and are great for the scalp too. Tinned fish is fine, by the way.

• Dairy products such as cheese and yogurt have stacks of protein for strong, healthy hair-growth and glowing skin.

• Milk is protein-packed too. Make smoothies or shakes by blending milk with banana and berries if you don't like it the way it comes.

• Dark green veg, such as spinach and broccoli, might not be your favourite parts of a meal, but they're packed with vitamins A, C and iron, and can give hair a healthy gloss.

• Nuts like cashews, brazils and almonds provide protein and zinc, a mineral your skin and hair love.

• Lean red meat is the best source of iron (an iron deficiency can make your skin very pale and your nails brittle too). If you're vegetarian you can still get your iron from wholemeal breads and cereals, eggs (especially the yolks), leafy dark green veg, dried apricots, and beans and pulses (a bowlful of lentil soup is perfect).

• Peanut butter, a great source of protein and vitamin A, helps to keep skin supple (a vitamin A deficiency can lead to dry skin and hair).

• Lean chicken is virtually all protein, and it's stuffed with B vitamins and minerals too.

• Seafood, a source of iron and zinc, helps to brighten skin and guard against those white spots on nails.

• Beans and pulses (like the chickpeas in houmous) are rich in protein.

• Peppers, strawberries, tomatoes and kiwis pack a punch of vitamin C.

• Eggs are packed with protein and vitamin B12, which make hair gorgeously shiny and soft. It doesn't matter how you eat yours — just eat them!

• And to drink? Don't forget that nothing beats water — add a squeeze of fresh fruit juice if you want to pep it up.

Three tips to steal

Dannii Minogue makes her own vitamin-packed juices. You do need a juicer to turn crunchy fruit, such as apples and pears, into a drink, but you can easily squeeze oranges with a citrus squeezer to make your own fresh juice for breakfast.

Actress Amanda Seyfried loves blueberries, so she pops them into delicious shakes. You can also freeze your shakes for delicious, all-natural lollies all summer long.

Don't deny yourself treats. Life really is too short for that, and it'll only make you want them all the more. Cheryl Cole tucks into a big fry-up at weekends, and there's nothing wrong with enjoying dessert if you're having three healthy meals a day.

How to wrap a present ... gorgeously

Any gift feels more exciting when you've taken the
time to wrap it beautifully ...

Basic wrapping

Most gifts can be wrapped with this simple
technique. Take a sheet of wrapping paper and place the present
face down in the middle of it. Bring the two longer sides over it and
secure with tape. Now fold in the corners of the two shorter ends
to make triangular shapes, then bring them towards you and stick
with tape at their tips. Toning or contrasting ribbon gives a lovely
finishing flourish.

Now to get personal

Use coloured tissue paper instead of wrapping paper. It comes
in dazzling colours, can be decorated with stuck-on sparkles or
sequins, and is especially good for oddly shaped gifts. If it's too
transparent, use a layer of white paper underneath.

• A layer of shiny, see-through cellophane looks great layered
over tissue or crepe paper.

• Plain brown wrapping paper has an eco-chic vibe – you can jazz
it up with a stamper and ink, or even paint a design on it (before you
wrap your gift, of course). Or you can decorate it by doodling on it
with a black fine-nibbed pen.

• Round or cylindrical presents look great wrapped

like Christmas crackers. Use ribbon to secure each end, and fluff out the paper, perhaps cutting a zigzag edge.

• A tiny present will be easier to wrap if you can find a little box for it first.

• Shiny makes a striking alternative to matt paper — look for shimmery silver, gold or jewel-coloured foils.

• The Japanese have a name for the art of wrapping gifts in fabric — *furoshiki*. You can use any fabric scraps or even a gorgeous vintage silk scarf, so long as you check it's okay to use first! Just gather the fabric round your gift and secure it with a ribbon.

• Curl thin, shiny ribbon by running it very carefully along a scissor blade.

• Keep old wrapping paper to re-use — you can iron out creases on a very low setting (a hot iron will scorch it).

• If you're the perfectionist type, use double-sided tape instead of normal sticky tape so you can't see it.

• Make your own gift tag with card and an ink stamper design. It'll look so good, you'll almost want to keep it yourself ...

How to make scrumptious chocolate brownies

There are times when only a brownie will do. Soft, fudgy and deeply chocolate-y, could anything be nicer to pop into your lunchbox or munch on when you come home from school?

What you need

- 190 g soft unsalted butter
- 190 g dark chocolate (one that has at least 70% cocoa solids works well – an even higher percentage is fine too)
- 250 g caster sugar
- 100 g plain flour
- 3 eggs
- 1 teaspoon vanilla essence
- a pinch of salt.

What to do

1. Preheat the oven to 180 °C, 350 °F or gas mark 4. Line a deep baking tray or brownie pan with greaseproof paper, making sure it goes up the sides too.

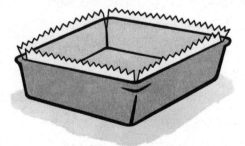

2. In a heavy-based pan, melt your chocolate and butter together on a low heat. Stir every now and then until it's runny and delicious. Let it cool a little (otherwise the eggy mixture will 'scramble' when you add it).

3. In a bowl, beat the eggs, sugar and vanilla essence until combined. Add to the slightly cooled chocolate mixture and stir together.

4. Now add the flour, salt and mix well. Pour it into your lined brownie pan and bake for around 25 minutes.

5. Using an oven glove, carefully remove the pan from the oven — ask an adult to help you with this bit. You'll know your brownies are ready when the top is firm, but an inserted skewer comes out slightly sticky from the gooey middle.

6. Leave to cool in the pan for a while before cutting into squares. Allow the brownie squares to cool fully on a wire rack, then dust lightly with icing sugar.

Other things do with your brownies ... • Warm them slightly and serve with vanilla ice cream.

• Pile them up on a plate and poke a birthday cake candle in each for an alternative (and possibly more delicious than usual) birthday cake. Gold candles look especially good.

• Add a handful of chopped walnuts to your mixture if you like them (make sure no one is allergic before you pass them round).

• Invite your friends over and cut them up into small cubes (the brownies that is). Use wooden skewers or toothpicks to dip them into a chocolate fondue. *Mmmm ...*

How to feel gorgeous inside

Great skin, hair and clothes all make you feel good – but nothing's as powerful as feeling truly gorgeous in your head and your heart. But ... how? These ten mottos can help to make you feel truly relaxed and at one with who you are. Feel free to make up your own, though – whatever works for you.

I'll deal with problems calmly – and not worry about the stuff that doesn't matter. It's hard to feel gorgeous when your head's stuffed with niggles and worries. So, if something needs to be tackled, then do it – you'll feel miles better afterwards. If you feel someone's treated you unfairly, say so, and if you've been grumbling to your friends about something irritating, but trivial, then make a conscious decision to let it go. Think of it as spring-cleaning your mind.

I'll accept my mistakes and move on. No point in going over and over something you wish you'd done differently, as it'll only hold you back. As Miley Cyrus puts it: 'I always say the minute I stop making mistakes is the minute I stop learning, and I've learned a lot.'

I won't hold grudges. So someone hurt your feelings ages ago? If she's tried to make amends, then it's time to forgive and forget. You'll feel so much better for it.

I'll stop criticizing myself and learn to love my best features. Are you always complaining about your hair, your skin or the shape of your nose? Putting yourself down can turn into a habit. Tyra Banks from *America's Next Top Model* suggests taking a good look at yourself in the mirror: 'Really look and spend some time there. Find one thing that you find beautiful about yourself … and celebrate that.'

I'll make sure I have time for thinking and dreaming. When you have a packed schedule, you can find yourself rushing from one thing to the next with no time to think. It's important to have the chance to chill out.

I'll keep secrets and promises – always. Blabbing them might be fun in a giggly, 'Did you hear this?' kind of way, but you'll feel guilty and mean afterwards.

I won't take people for granted. When life's busy, it's easy for friends to fall by the wayside. Keeping in touch only takes minutes, and a quick text or call makes a buddy know you're thinking of her.

I'll always remember that I can ask for help and support. For actress Vanessa Hudgens, that's her mum and her mates: 'If I'm having a bad day, I'll be straight on the phone to my momma and then my friends.'

I'll remember how lucky I am. You might feel that everyone has a better time and more opportunities than you do. But what about all the good things in your life? Try to focus on the positive, and learn to accept and love the person you are.

I won't always put myself first. This might mean sometimes agreeing to watch the film your friend wants to see, rather than the one you would have chosen, or helping out someone in your family because you know it'll make a big difference to them. It's just about being generous and a **Good Person**, which is really what inner gorgeousness is all about.

How to fix a beauty blunder

So you've bodged your eyes or your lips looks weird … it's one of those 'Eek!' moments. But don't worry as virtually any blunder can be sorted in a jiffy. Here's how:

My mascara's gone clumpy. Just wipe your mascara wand clean of product, then use it to carefully brush through your lashes to whisk away any blobs.

I've got mascara flecks or eyeliner smudges everywhere. Dip a cotton bud in a little moisturizer or make-up remover and use it to wipe away. Then blend with a dry cotton bud.

My eyes are scary. Been a bit heavy handed with the eye shadow? If you're in a hurry there might not be time to cleanse it off and start again. First, see if you can gently wipe some away with a cotton-wool pad, or tone it down by sweeping over it with a clean blusher brush. If that's not enough to fade the colour, brush a little loose powder over the top.

I've gone overboard with blusher. Light wiping over with a cotton-wool pad might be enough to reduce the colour. If you still look flushed rather than rosy, brush over some loose powder.

My lipstick's wonky. It might be easiest to wipe it away with tissue and start again. Or whisk away the wobbles with a cotton bud dipped in make-up remover, then re-do the outline of your lips. If they still look uneven, you're probably using too strong or dark a shade — natural colours are easier to work with, as minor wobbles won't show.

I've over-darkened my brows. Just brush them through with an old, but clean, toothbrush, or — if that's not enough — wipe over with a cotton-wool pad and a little make-up remover. Then blot the brow area with tissue and comb brows back into place — without adding more colour.

I've splodged my nails. Nail polish looks like your cat applied it? Dip a cotton bud in nail polish remover, then use to wipe away the stray blob. Dry off with a small piece of clean tissue.

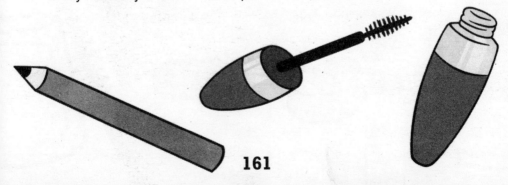

I've decided I don't like my nail polish colour. If you don't have time to remove and reapply, try painting over — either with a paler, sheer colour, or with a coat of sparkly polish on top. An iffy colour can look great with a dash of added glitter.

I've overdone everything! Ah, the too-much-of-a-good-thing situation. With make-up, it's always best to emphasize either your eyes or lips — playing up both just looks too much. So use one of the toning-down tricks mentioned above, allowing your best feature to shine.

To avoid those 'eek' moments ...
Build up colour gradually and blend, blend, blend. Remember, it's easy to add more if you want to.

Apply make-up in natural daylight if you can, or at least check it in daylight before you leave the house.

If you're heading out in a hurry, stick to easy-to-wear colours that you know suit you. Best to keep your make-up experiments for when you have tons of time.

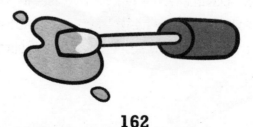

How to curl and straighten your hair

Whether you want super-straight hair, luscious waves or bouncy curls, with a little practice you'll soon be able to create fabulous special-occasion styles. Do remember to use a curling iron or straighteners on dry (not damp) hair, and take care not to burn yourself!

Remember too much heat can stress out your hair, so keep yours healthy by:

• Not reaching for your curling iron or straighteners every day.

• Using a heat protective spray or lotion every time, plus a leave-in conditioner once or twice a week.

• Curling or straightening each section of hair just once, rather than going over and over it.

• Avoiding using heated appliances if your hair is feeling coarse or dry.

For super-straight hair

Start by clipping back the top layer of hair and straightening the underneath sections (you'll get best results if you glide the straighteners slowly along your hair). Then unclip, and work through the rest of your hair, section by section. A squirt of spray shine will add extra gloss.

For loose waves

Start straightening a small section of hair from the roots. Once you reach halfway down, flip the straighteners upside down so your hair is coming out of the top. Carry on straightening slowly. For looser waves, gently brush out or run through your hair with your fingers.

For crinkly waves

Here's a lovely way to make waves that doesn't involve heat. Wash your hair in the evening and use a leave-in conditioner, then divide your hair into several plaits that you'll sleep in. Two plaits will produce big waves, four will make medium ones, and lots will produce a crinkly effect. In the morning, undo your plaits and run your fingers through to separate them.

For bouncy curls

It's best to curl your hair in small sections. The smaller the sections, the tighter the curls will be (you'll need plenty of time and patience to create a whole head of corkscrew curls, and it'll be a lot easier if you can persuade a friend to do the back for you). When your curls are done, you can either 'relax' them by running your fingers through before they've completely cooled, or define and add shine with a quick squirt of serum.

For extra volume

Hold a section of hair taut and upwards from your head. Start straightening from the roots towards the ceiling, then bring the section of hair back down and carry on straightening normally.

How to pep up your look in five minutes (or less)

Beautifying needn't be fussy. Sometimes, one simple trick makes all the difference. Try these ...

Freshen up ... Wet a flannel with very warm (not hot) water and press over your face, then splash on lots of cold water. This revs up your circulation, gives you a glow and makes you feel more perky too.

Change your hair parting ... It's the quickest way to a new look (and no one will guess what you've done).

Hint of a tint ... For flattering colour and shine, tinted lip gloss is a genius wear-anywhere product to keep in your bag. If it's creamy rather than greasy, you can stroke on a little as cheek colour too.

Tame flyaway hair ... Just spritz a flat brush with hairspray, then smooth over those stray strands.

Try an eyeliner flick ... For this you'll need liquid eyeliner that comes with a tiny brush, or an eyeliner pen (the new gel-type liners glide on beautifully). It's easier to apply if you pull your skin slightly taut, by gently stretching it from the outer corner. Starting at the inner corner, carefully draw a fine line as close as possible to your upper lashes. Widen the line slightly as you reach the outer corner of the eye, and finish with a little flick.

Hide under-eye shadows ... Brighten your look by dotting on a little concealer, then carefully blend with a finger. Use sparingly though — too much looks clogged-up and obvious.

Make your eyes look bigger ... For this, you need two toning shades of eye shadow. Apply the paler colour over your lid, then the darker one along the socket line to create the illusion of depth. Blend together, so that the two colours merge.

Make your lips look fuller ... Apply a warm, pinky-nude lipstick, then add a little gloss to the centre of your bottom lip. *Voilà!*

Three tips to steal

Model Amber le Bon, whose mum Yasmin le Bon was one of the original supermodels, has a favourite party trick: 'Curling my hair — I think it looks really feminine. I can't reach the back of my head though, so Tallulah [her little sis] does it when she's in a good mood.'

If model Georgia May Jagger only has time to apply one product, it's a moisturizer with a high SPF. That way, she knows her fair skin is protected and kept super-soft.

'I used to use bronzer everywhere,' says Leona Lewis, 'but you're not supposed to do that. Brush it along your temples and under your cheekbones — places that give that sun-kissed glow.' Take care not to overdo it — you're looking for a subtle shimmer, not a full-on metallic effect.

How to sing beautifully

Always dreamt of being able to sing? Like most things in life, practising makes a huge difference, as long as you're doing it the right way. Follow these tips and you'll soon be hitting all the right notes, gorgeously ...

Privacy. First of all, it's important that you have somewhere to practise without other people commenting every five seconds. You need to be able to focus, and it's hard to do that with an audience you don't feel ready for ...

Posture. The way you hold yourself affects the sound you make. Stand straight with your feet shoulder-width apart and your shoulders and arms relaxed.

Breathe. Singing is a little like playing a wind instrument, in that it's important to breathe from your diaphragm (the muscle at the bottom your rib cage). This enables you to take in more air and let it out in a controlled, steady way as you sing. You'll know you're working your diaphragm when your stomach goes out as you breathe in.

Warm up. Think of your voice as a delicate instrument. Warming up protects it from damage. Start with some relaxed deep breaths and humming, then do some scales to an 'ah' sound, or sing 'do-re-mi'. 'I do a 30-minute warm-up every single day,' says Lady Gaga.

Practise. If you sing every day, you'll be amazed at how quickly you improve. You don't have to sing alone either – joining a choir or singing with friends makes it even more fun.

Be inspired. Listen to your favourite singers, but remember that everyone's voice is unique. If you're true to your own vocal range, rather than forcing it or straining for notes, you'll soon develop your own personal style.

Listen. Record and listen to your singing – it's a great motivator, as you'll hear yourself getting better all the time.

Create. You could even start writing your own material. 'If you sing with enough passion and emotion, you can turn anything into a song,' believes Florence Welch.

How to care for pierced ears

Newly pierced ears need extra TLC to lessen the chances of redness, infection and other nasties. Here's how to help them heal ...

Avoid touching your earrings or piercings unless you're cleaning them. Even then, wash your hands first.

For six weeks after piercing, gently cleanse the fronts and backs of your lobes with cotton-wool balls and ear care lotion. It's important to do this three times a day — if you think you'll forget, at the start of each week, write down the days and tick each time you've done it. So each day should have three ticks before you go to bed.

Remember to carefully rotate your earrings by a half-turn two or three times a day.

It'll take at least six weeks for your piercings to heal, so you'll need to keep your starter earrings in. Don't be tempted to take them out earlier, no matter how desperate you are to change them. Switching earrings too soon, when the area is still tender, is a prime cause of infection.

Try to keep shampoo and conditioner away from your newly pierced ears, and make sure that any blobs of product are gently showered away.

During this healing time, watch out for any soreness, redness, swelling or oozy stuff … and if any of that happens, see your doctor (without taking out your earrings).

Once all's healed, by all means switch your earrings – but avoid heavy dangly types as they can pull down on the ear and make the hole really long (ew).

How to shop without blowing all your cash

What every girl needs to grab those bargains ...

A plan. It's a good idea to know roughly what you're looking for before you set out, and how much you'll allow yourself to spend. Do a bit of research first by checking out stores' websites to see what's new.

A positive mood. It's best not to go shopping if you're feeling tired or low, as you might find yourself buying things just to cheer yourself up. Those 'blue' days are better spent nesting all cosily at home (see p. 31-33).

A shopping outfit. Non-fiddly clothes (and shoes) that are easy to whip off and on in changing rooms.

A sassy friend. Some mates egg you on to spend all your money in the first five minutes. Others are, let's say ... more cautious. While it's not much fun shopping with a friend who reckons everything is a bad buy, you need someone with a touch of sensibleness about her. She shouldn't be too pushy either — otherwise you might find yourself buying stuff that's more to her taste than yours. If you're looking for something specific, it's easier to track it down with just one friend, rather than hitting the shops with a big gang of mates.

Plenty of time. If you're in a rush, you're more likely to buy something without thinking it through. Small impulse buys are fun, but if it's cost you two weeks' pocket money you might regret it. If you're not sure, have a wander round some other shops first — you can always pop back later to buy it. It's harder to curb impulses if you're shopping online, so take extra care not to splurge madly.

Hawk-eyes. Bargains can be squirrelled out, especially at sale time. But you might have to rummage through acres of rubbish to find them.

A cool head. That means considering whether you really want an item before you splurge. Never be tempted to buy something just because it's cheap, it's there, and you don't want to go home empty-handed. Also, make sure it really does fit (saying, 'It's a bit too tight and it pinches, but it'll be okay,' doesn't mean it should be yours). Also consider when — and how — you'll wear it. Does it go with other stuff in your wardrobe, and does it feel 'right'? Do you not just like but **love** it?

Changing-room savvy. Always try things on before scampering towards the till, as pieces with zero 'hanger appeal' can look amazing on, while others can turn out to be disastrous even though they looked promising in the shop. It helps to have a friend to act as your handy assistant, fetching different sizes if you need them. Don't forget to check your back view too, and get your friend's (honest) opinion. Sales assistants *always* say something looks good …

And if you change your mind?
Although shops don't have to take things back unless they're faulty or 'not fit for purpose', most do have a returns policy. This means they'll give you a refund, exchange or credit note (which you

can 'spend' on items to the same value) as long as you have the original receipt.

Usually, you have 28 days after buying to return an item to the shop. It must be unused and in perfect condition and in its original packaging, so don't rip tags off clothes, wear shoes outside, or take the cellophane wrapper off DVDs until you're sure. Some items, such as earrings, are often non-returnable, and you won't be able to take back any make-up or beauty products if they've been opened. Understandably, no one will want that body butter once you've poked your fingers in it.

How to be strong, fit and active

Everyone knows how important it is to be fit and active. But as well as helping to keep your body at a healthy weight, did you know that exercising has loads of other benefits too?

• You'll sleep better if you've been active during the day.

• Exercise boosts your body's systems, improving your circulation and helping your body to digest food — it can help improve your skin too.

• Aerobic (or continuous) exercise is a great mood-lifter and stress-buster. Try running, swimming and cycling to chase the blues away.

• Although it might make you feel more tired at first, you'll soon discover that regular exercise gives you more energy.

• If you get involved with a team sport, it's sociable, fun and great for your confidence too.

It's official — exercise really does make you happier!

Great ... so what shall I choose?

The key to keeping up exercise, rather than getting bored and quitting, is discovering something you love. So feel free to try out a whole range of activities such as volleyball, hockey, netball, cross-country running, football, tennis, swimming, badminton and gymnastics.

I don't feel confident about starting on my own ...

Ask a friend if she'd like to join you. Research shows that you're far more likely to keep it up if you have a fitness buddy for company. You'll tend to push yourself further and might even get a teeny bit competitive!

So how should I get started?

You don't need to rush out and spend a fortune on kit. For most activities, all you need is light clothing and a good pair of trainers. Start gently, giving your body the chance to get used to exercise: if you push yourself too hard, you might lose confidence or even hurt or strain yourself. It's more important that you exercise regularly – around three times a week – for at least twenty minutes each time. Then, as your fitness improves, you can start to set yourself goals. Soon, you'll start to feel so good that you won't want to give up.

How can I keep my energy up?

If you're becoming more active your body needs quality fuel – which means never skipping breakfast. Protein (like eggs), plus wholegrains such as cereal or toast provide long-lasting energy. For snacks, go for fruit, nuts, crackers and cheese instead of sugary or salt-laden nibbles. Ideally, you should have an energy-boosting snack (oatcakes and a banana are ideal) a couple of hours before exercising. But don't run, swim or play sport immediately after a meal or you might feel queasy or get cramps.

But I'm not really the sporty type ...

You don't need to be. Teams sports aren't for everyone, and anything that gets your body moving — even walking the dog — is doing you good. Whatever you choose, it should never feel like a chore.

Three tips to steal

Before a tour, daily dance rehearsals keep Katy Perry in shape. So why not pop on your favourite song and get moving? She also takes a skipping rope in her suitcase: 'There's a rhythm to it,' she says. 'It's like dancing. I can double jump, I can cross, I can do it all.'

Actress Billie Piper pulls on her jogging bottoms and goes for a long run. If you're just starting out, try alternating walking with jogging until your stamina improves. 'I'll walk for a minute and a half, then I run for a minute, then sprint for a minute,' says superfit star Anne Hathaway (this is called 'interval training'). Remember to stay hydrated by sipping water.

You don't have to stick to one thing. Actress Kate Hudson keeps things interesting by mixing it up: cycling, canoeing and gym workouts are all part of her active life.

How to 'upcycle' – gorgeously

Upcycling means taking something old, broken or that you don't want anymore ... and turning it into a fantastic new thing. It's cheap, it's creative and you'll know that whatever you make is unique. Here are some quick projects to get you started.

A beautiful silky cushion for your bed ... If you have, or can borrow, a sewing machine, you can easily revamp a ratty old cushion by making a new cover with two old silk scarves. It doesn't matter if front and back don't match – in fact, using contrasting scarves means you can turn your cushion over for a different look. Use the old cushion cover as pattern to make sure you cut your scarves to the right size. If you like, you can stitch on embellishments like sparkly beads and sequins.

(Almost) instant art ... Pick up an art board (they're often sold cheaply in bargain bookstores) and dig out some gorgeous old fabric to display. Again, a silk scarf is ideal – but a piece from an old dress or skirt will work too if it's beautiful enough. Position your fabric on your board the way you like it, then fold it over the back and trim the excess. You'll need to leave enough to attach it to the back of the board – a staple gun's the easiest way to do this, but do get an adult to help you. When it comes to the corners of the fabric, fold them over in the way you would wrap a gift, and staple these too, nice and neatly. Now just put it on display. Beautiful.

Rescued beads ... Broken beaded necklaces can be given new life and turned into a bracelet. You can mix up materials such as glass, ceramic, plastic and wood – the most interesting bracelets are often made from unusual combinations. The simplest way to re-string them is by using elastic – just knot firmly when you're done, making sure it's of a size that won't slip off your wrist.

To make a necklace, buy some fine beading wire – the kind that's ready to thread and has a little screw-on clasp attached. Then thread on your beads in whatever pattern you fancy. If you don't have much broken jewellery, ask friends to dig out theirs, put all your finds together and have a re-threading session together.

Jeans genius ... Just because your jeans are ripped doesn't mean you should sling them away. After all, what girl can't use a pair of denim cut-offs? Try on your jeans and mark how short you'd like them with a piece of chalk. Then take them off and cut them carefully with tough scissors. You could hem them, or simply fray the edges with your scissors. If you like, customize them with little sewn-on patches, and if you want them to look even more vintage, place them on a hard surface and give them a rub with some sandpaper.

Dyeing for a change ... The easiest way to revamp old clothes is by dyeing them – and the best way to do that is in the washing machine. (Always follow the packet instructions carefully.)

The best things to dye are made from cotton, linen or viscose fabrics — to find out what your item is made from, check the label. Other fabrics might take on the dye, but not be as vibrant as you'd like. You can't dye wool, silk, polyester or 'dry clean only' fabrics in the washing machine (use a hand-wash dye instead).

White or pale fabrics will give better results than darker colours (for instance, if you try to dye a red garment blue, it will come out a purple or burgundy shade, in the same way that paint colours mix). Plain fabrics work better than patterns, as the design will probably still show through. You can't dye anything paler than its original colour.

As you can't entirely predict how a garment will come out, it's best not to dye anything precious.

Got all that? Now you're ready to dye. Just pop your dye in the drum of the machine, plus your dry garment. Wash it at a 40° cotton setting and, when it's done, dry it away from direct heat (hanging it up is ideal. Draping it over a radiator: not ideal).

Switch on the washing machine again (on the same 40° cycle) to get rid of any traces of dye. Otherwise your whole family's stuff might come out bright blue and they won't be best pleased!

As for your own dyed item, it's best to wash it separately in case some of the dye comes out and tints other clothes.

One pack of machine dye is usually enough to dye something around the weight of a pair of jeans. If you're dying something smaller and lighter in weight, ask a friend if she has something she'd like to chuck in the machine too.

Other dye tricks to try ...

• If something's faded, you can refresh it by dyeing it in a colour that's close to its original shade. However, for an even result, you should use a pre-dye product first.

• You can also buy special dye to re-colour your shoes.

• You don't just have to dye clothes. Changing the colour of a cushion cover, a duvet cover or throw is a cheap and cheerful way to make-over your bedroom. But do stop short of dyeing the dog.

How to have star quality

Star quality is what makes you stand out from the crowd. It ensures that people remember you and gives you that extra 'zing' — yet it's very hard to pin down exactly what it is. It's not just about looks — even the most classically beautiful people can lack star quality. Yet when someone has it, you really know because you can't take your eyes off them. They're mesmerizing.

In fact, everyone can have star quality, but sometimes it can take a little nurturing to truly shine. The crucial thing is to believe in yourself, and never listen to that little negative voice that puts doubts in your head. When you have rock-solid self-belief, you can really go for what you want in life, and give it your all.

Seven steps to fabulousness ...

Discover your special talent. Sometimes, you know exactly what you want to do in life. But lots of people take some time to get there. Make it easier to uncover that talent by trying out as many new experiences as you can, and grabbing any opportunity that comes your way. Whether it's sport, music, fashion or art — or something else entirely — you'll know when you find it, as it'll just feel 'right'.

Do something for the right reasons ... not just for the attention or because you want to be famous, but in a way that makes it meaningful to you.

186

Dare to take that first step. Usually, that's the hardest bit, because it's unknown, and what we don't know scares us the most. For instance, if you're shy, walking into a party is more nerve-racking than actually being there and chatting to people. Once you've been brave and walked in, things only get easier. So take a deep breath and do it. You'll feel really proud of yourself and that'll make your confidence soar.

Remember that most people want you to succeed. To truly shine, bear in mind that they're on your side and cheering you on. Do your best to make them proud of you – but above all, do it for yourself.

Always be willing to learn. It's great to know you're talented, but a mistake to think you know it all and can't get any better at what you do. So take advice, listen to people you trust, and be prepared to work your socks off to be the best you can be.

Have fun ... and be able to laugh at yourself. When things go wrong, remember that little set-backs can make you stronger, and you always learn from them.

On the other hand ... don't lose your own identity and style. Only you know how you want to be, and you should have the last word on that. After all, it's what makes you unique and not just a copy of someone else. While actress Jennifer Lawrence feels she's still learning her craft, she says: 'There are actresses who build themselves, then there are actresses who are built by others. I want to build myself.' Jennifer Lopez puts it this way: 'I want to progress as a singer and songwriter, and produce movies and everything. So there'll be no time when I feel I've done it all.'

A gorgeous girl's manifesto

Here are some little life rules to keep things sweet:

Gorgeous girls ...

... make time for a friend when she's feeling down,
and don't make up excuses not to see her

... know that true gorgeousness isn't all about looks,
and don't primp and preen every time they pass a mirror

... have fun experimenting with clothes,
and don't feel obliged to latch onto every trend

... love giving presents,
and don't hanker after what everyone else has

... have a beautiful smile,
and don't pose and pout

... like nothing better than a good laugh,
and don't take themselves too seriously

... know their own minds,
and don't follow the crowd

... look great without make-up,
and don't freak out if a favourite lippie is lost

... know what their best features are,
and don't put themselves down

... look for the positive qualities in people,
and don't criticize people for being different.

Who's got the last word on gorgeousness?
20 tips for instant fabulousness from girls in the know ...

 'Wearing my hair differently or changing my style of dress is playing dress-up. I don't take it too seriously' — singer, Mariah Carey

 'Set yourself realistic goals. This could be running your first mile or taking part in a 5 kilometre race' — runner, Paula Radcliffe

'I never skip breakfast, no matter what. It's the most important meal of the day, and it's my favourite to cook' — actress, Cameron Diaz

'There's no definition of beauty, but when you can see someone's spirit coming through, something unexplainable, that's beautiful to me' — actress, Liv Tyler

'How wonderful it is that nobody need wait a single moment before starting to improve the world' — Anne Frank, author of Anne Frank: *The Diary of a Young Girl*

'I feel very adventurous. There are so many doors to be opened, and I'm not afraid to look behind them' — Hollywood icon, Elizabeth Taylor

 'Every once in a while, a girl has to indulge herself' — actress, Sarah Jessica Parker

☆ 'I'm happy, and I think happiness is what makes you pretty' — actress, Drew Barrymore

♡ 'I'm not going to change my teeth or get a nose job. That manufactured perfection does nothing for me' — model and actress, Rosie Huntington-Whiteley

☆ 'I was bullied at school. My advice would be to tell someone you trust straight away' — singer, Jessie J

♡ 'Mum used to wear these beautiful 30s tea dresses with a pop T-shirt, a pair of boots … that's exactly what I do, and lots of girls do now. Mix it all up' — fashion designer, Stella McCartney

☆ 'Some people say I have an attitude — maybe I do. But I think that you have to. You have to believe in yourself when no one else does' — tennis star, Venus Williams

♡ 'I became my own stylist by not knowing any better' — actress, Blake Lively

☆ 'Beauty is how you feel inside, and it reflects in your eyes. It's not something physical' — actress, Sophia Loren

'I cannot do everything, but I can do something. I must not fail at the something I can do' — deaf-blind campaigner and activist, Helen Keller

'It's better to have a go at something than have regrets' — author, Jacqueline Wilson

'The more you trust your intuition, the more empowered you become, the stronger your become and the happier you become' — supermodel, Gisele Bundchen

'I think everything happens for a reason, so there's no such thing as fail' — actress, Mary-Kate Olsen

'Treat people with dignity and respect, even if you don't know them and even if you don't agree with them' — First Lady, Michelle Obama

And the very last word must go to actress, Kirsten Dunst ...

'The real secret to total gorgeousness is to believe in yourself, have self-confidence, and try to be secure in your decisions and thoughts.'